BROWNIE RECIPES

Edited by Carole Eberly

Cover & Illustrations by Gerry Wykes

Copyright 1983 **eberly press**
430 N. Harrison
E. Lansing, MI 48823
ISBN 0-932296-10-6

Welcome to Brownie Heaven

Our shelves are laden with the finest chocolate, the richest cream, the sweetest sugars, the loveliest walnuts and pecans. In the oven is a batch of Chocolate Mint Stick Brownies. Cooling near the window are pans of Coconut Topped Brownies and Apricot-Chocolate Brownies. A freshly whipped bowl of butter cream frosting waits near a batch of cooled Chocolate Butter Cream Brownies. There are, altogether, more than 170 brownie recipes made here.

In case you're wondering, all scales are banned, all calorie counting books forbidden, and all waistbands are expandable. We encourage licking the beaters; snitching extra brownies is greatly rewarded.

The only thing lacking is your presence. Won't you join us?

FOR JOHN & JESSICA

BEFORE (READING THIS BOOK.)

Thank Yous

Thanks to all these wonderful people in *Brownie Recipes* who agreed to share their recipes with you. They are the kind of friendly people who'd invite you in for a cup of coffee and some brownies if you happened by their neighborhood. Their helpful comments and suggestions in putting this book together are deeply appreciated. Without them, there would be no *Brownie Recipes*.

Thank you, also, to the staff and management of the *Detroit Free Press* who allowed me to use their files in compiling this book. It was the *Free Press' Best Ever Brownie Recipe Contest* which provided the brainstorm for this book. Most of the recipes in this book came from the 1,500 entries it received; the remainder are from my own files.

Thank you, again, to everyone. It's been a fun project.

— Carole Eberly

AFTER (READING THIS BOOK.)

Cream Cheese Brownies

(It's a good, moist brownie–doesn't need frosting, and doesn't stay around very long either.)

1 package (4 ounces) Baker's German sweet chocolate
5 tablespoons butter or margarine
1 package (3 ounces) cream cheese, softened
1 cup sugar
3 eggs
1 tablespoon all-purpose flour
1½ teaspoons vanilla
½ teaspoon baking powder
¼ teaspoon salt
½ cup all-purpose flour
½ cup coarsely chopped nuts

Melt chocolate and 3 tablespoons of the butter in a small saucepan over very low heat, stirring constantly. Cool.

Blend remaining butter with cream cheese until softened. Gradually add ¼ cup of the sugar, beating well. Blend in 1 egg, 1 tablespoon flour and ½ teaspoon vanilla. Set aside.

Beat remaining 2 eggs until thick and light in color. Gradually add remaining ¾ cup sugar, beating until thickened. Add baking powder, salt and ½ cup flour.

Blend in cooled chocolate mixture, nuts and 1 teaspoon vanilla.

Spread about half of the chocolate batter in greased 8 or 9-inch square pan.

Add cheese mixture, spreading evenly.

Top with tablespoons of remaining chocolate batter.

Zigzag a spatula through batter to marble.

Bake at 350° for 35-40 minutes, or until top springs back when lightly pressed in center. Cool. Cut into bars or squares.

(I double this recipe and bake it in a 9x13-inch pan. I just bake it a little longer. I also omit the nuts sometimes because my children aren't too fond of them.)

Peg Tarpoff
East Lansing

Pecan Pie Brownies

(This has been a favorite brownie recipe of mine for many years. It's sinfully rich! The original recipe called for walnuts. I like pecans better. It's my favorite because it's an elegant dessert for any meal–even brunch. It can be baked in a 10-inch pie pan and served with ice cream or whipped cream. Delicious!)

> 1 18½-ounce package dark chocolate cake mix*
> ½ cup butter, melted**
> 1 egg
> ½ cup packed brown sugar
> 1½ cups dark corn syrup (I prefer Karo)
> 1 teaspoon vanilla
> 3 eggs
> 1 cup chopped pecans

*Yellow cake mix can be used for light brownies.
**You can substitute good quality margarine.

Reserve ⅔ cup cake mix for filling.

Combine remaining dry cake mix, butter and 1 egg; mix well. Press into greased 9x13-inch pan. Bake in preheated 350°-oven for 15-20 minutes or until lightly browned.

Meanwhile, combine ⅔ cup reserved cake mix, ½ cup brown sugar, Karo syrup, vanilla and 3 eggs. Beat at medium speed for 1-2 minutes. Pour filling over partically baked crust; sprinkle with pecans.

Return to oven and bake for 30-35 minutes or until filling is set. Cool.

Cut into 36 bars.

Mary L. Richards
GRAND RAPIDS

Buttercream Brownies Deluxe

Brownies–Step 1

1 cup sugar
3 tablespoons cocoa
2 eggs, slightly beaten
1 teaspoon vanilla
¾ cup flour
6 tablespoons butter, melted
½ cup chopped walnuts, if desired

Mix sugar and cocoa. Add eggs and vanilla; beat until smooth. Stir in flour. Add butter and mix well. Add nuts, if desired. Turn into buttered 8-inch square pan. Bake at 350° for 25-30 minutes. Cool slightly.

Topping–Step 2

While brownies cool slightly, brown **¼ cup soft butter** over medium heat. Blend with **2 cups sifted confectioners sugar**. Blend in **2 tablespoons cream** and **1 teaspoon vanilla**. Spread on brownies.

Finishing Touch–Step 3

Melt **1 square (1 ounce) unsweetened chocolate** and **1 tablespoon butter**. When cooled, spread very thin coating over icing. Yield: 16 2-inch squares, or cut in "fingers."

Doris Grandy
BIRMINGHAM

Cracked Top Brownies

¾ cup cocoa
½ teaspoon baking soda
⅔ cup vegetable oil
½ cup boiling water
2 cups sugar
2 eggs
1½ cup flour
1 teaspoon vanilla
¼ teaspoon salt

Stir cocoa and soda; blend in ⅓ cup vegetable oil. Add boiling water; stir till it thickens. Stir in sugar, eggs, and remaining ⅓ cup oil. Stir till smooth. Add flour, vanilla and salt; blend completely. Pour into a greased 13x9-inch pan. Bake at 350° for 35-40 minutes.

When cool, push top layer lightly to crack; then dust with powdered sugar.

Peggy Day
MARQUETTE

YEAH, I ESCAPED FROM THE FEDERAL
PAN THREE TIMES.

Brownies a l'Orange

(This recipe has been named the Official Brownie of the 1983 Annual Cummins Fourth of July picnic!)

> **Candied orange zest (recipe follows),**
>   **about ⅔ cup, divided**
> **1 cup flour**
> **1⅔ cups sugar**
> **2 grade A large eggs**
> **4 ounces unsweetened chocolate, chopped**
> **1½ sticks unsalted butter,**
>   **in 1-inch pieces**
> **1 teaspoon vanilla extract**

Place butter and chocolate pieces in saucepan, set in large pan in which water has been brought to simmer. Melt butter and chocolate together until smooth.

In large mixing bowl, beat eggs until light yellow. Stir in sugar and lukewarm chocolate mixture. Sift flour over and blend until all flour is moistened. Add vanilla.

Working quickly, spread one-half brownie mixture in buttered or greased 9x9-inch or 9x13-inch baking pan. Sprinkle one-half orange zest evenly over brownie mixture, and cover with second half of brownie mixture. Garnish surface with remaining zest.

Bake in oven preheated to 350° for 25 minutes. (The larger pan will produce a crisper brownie.) Let cool in pan. Cut into squares.

Candied Orange Zest

1 medium navel orange
¼ cup sugar
½ cup water
More water for boiling zest

With vegetable peeler, remove zest (colored part of peel) from orange. Cut into fine julienne strips.

Place zest strips in saucepan and cover with cold water. Bring to boil; drain. Repeat boiling process; drain.

Place ¼ cup sugar and ½ cup water in saucepan and simmer over low to medium heat until sugar is dissolved to form a thin syrup. Reduce heat to low, place zest in syrup and simmer slowly (do not boil) until sugar is absorbed, about 30 minutes. Remove zest to waxed paper sheet, separate strands with knife tip, and let dry.

(Candied zest can be stored in a covered jar and refrigerated for several weeks. It's delicious alone or as a topping on ice cream and other desserts.)

Kathleen M. Cummins
BIRMINGHAM

9

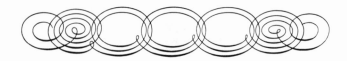

Pawtuckett Brownie Fingers

*(These are, by far, the best-loved brownies by my family and friends.
They goes into all gift packages that we ship out. They also freeze well.)*

1 cup sugar
2½ tablespoons Drost cocoa
¾ cup flour
½ teaspoon baking powder
½ teaspoon salt
1 teaspoon vanilla
1 cup chopped nuts
3 eggs, separated
½ cup melted butter

Mix sugar and cocoa. In a separate bowl, mix together the balance
of dry ingredients.

Beat egg whites till stiff. Beat egg yolks until lemon-colored. Add
egg yolks to sugar and cocoa. Fold in egg whites. Fold in flour mixture
and butter alternately. Add vanilla and nuts.

Bake in a greased 9x9-inch pan at 350° for 30 minutes–test as for
cake. Cool. Cut into fingers. Sprinkle with powdered sugar.

Irene S. Ross
BLOOMFIELD HILLS

❖❖Double Frosted Bourbon Brownies❖❖

(These brownies are excellent without bourbon. I only add bourbon when I make them as Christmas gifts.)

❖❖❖❖❖❖

¼ cup butter or margarine
2 squares unsweetened chocolate
2 eggs
1 cup sugar
½ cup flour
¼ teaspoon salt
1 teaspoon vanilla
1 package (6 ounces) real chocolate chips
4 tablespoons bourbon

White Frosting

½ cup soft butter
1 teaspoon vanilla
2 cups powdered sugar

Chocolate Glaze

1 square unsweetened chocolate
1 tablespoon butter

Over low heat melt butter and chocolate. Beat eggs until light. Beat in sugar until thick and lemon colored.

Add chocolate mixture, flour and salt. Mix well. Stir in vanilla and chocolate chips.

Pour into greased 8 or 9-inch square pan. Bake at 375° for 15-20 minutes, or until done.

With fork, gently poke holes in brownies and pour the bourbon over brownies. Cool.

Mix all frosting ingredients. Frost cool brownies. Put in refrigerator 30 minutes to solidfy.

For glaze, melt chocolate and butter. Drizzle over frosting layer, tilting pan to cover completely. Refrigerate briefly to set chocolate.

You can store these in the refrigerator, but remove 15-20 minutes before cutting.

This recipe can be doubled for a 9x13-inch pan, baking for 25-30 minutes. (Do not double the white frosting or chocolate chips–use 1½ times the amount called for in recipe.)

These brownies can be frozen. You can also add chopped walnuts, if desired.

Susan Adair
PLEASANT RIDGE

11

E-Z Hidden Easter Egg Baskets

(My junior brownie testers here at home–ages 2,5, and 30–enjoy making these as much as eating them.)

> 1 box brownie mix, plus ingredients
>   for making cake-like brownies
> 12 wafer-type wide flat-bottomed
>   ice cream cones
> 12 small milk chocolate Easter egg candies
>   (foil removed)
> 12 thin chocolate mint patties
> Green-tinted flaked or shredded coconut
> 12 thick licorice twists
>   (any flavor preferred)
> Assorted small jelly beans

Prepare mix as directed on package of cake-like brownies.

Fill each cone with scant ¼ cup prepared batter. (Use any remaining batter as desired.) To help prevent tipping over, place each cone in a separate cup of muffin tin. Place one chocolate candy in middle of batter of each filled cone. Bake at 350° for about 25-30 minutes, or until it tests done.

Place one chocolate mint patty on top of each baked brownie. Return cones to oven about 3 minutes, or until patties are softened. Remove cones to cooling racks and spread mint patty to cover top of brownie. Cool.

Sprinkle coconut "grass" into each cone to cover tops of each frosted brownie. Bend each licorice twist and push ends into sides of each "basket," forming "handle."

Fill each basket with a few jelly beans.

Rose Adams
DETROIT

Chocolate Rum Cream Brownies

½ cup (1 stick) butter or margarine
2 ounces (2 squares) unsweetened chocolate
1 cup sugar
2 eggs
¼ cup rum cream liqueur
1 teaspoon vanilla
½ cup flour
¼ teaspoon salt

Melt butter or margarine and chocolate together over hot water. Remove from heat and stir in sugar. Cool briefly.

Beat in eggs, mixing well after each addition.

Stir in rum cream and vanilla.

Blend in flour and salt, mixing well. If desired, add **½ cup chopped walnuts**.

Pour into a greased 8-inch square baking pan. Bake at 325° about 40 minutes. Remove from oven and cool 30 minutes. Cut into squares.

Tropical Brownies

½ cup shortening
2 squares unsweetened chocolate
1 cup sugar
2 eggs, well beaten
1 flat can crushed pineapple, drained
½ teaspoon vanilla
1 cup flour
½ teaspoon baking powder
¼ teaspoon soda
¼ teaspoon salt
½ cup chopped nuts

Method:

1. Melt shortening and chocolate in top of double boiler. Blend in sugar.

2. Remove from heat and blend in eggs, crushed pineapple and vanilla.

3. Sift together flour, baking powder, soda and salt. Add to pineapple mixture.

4. Stir in chopped nuts. Pour mixture into well-greased, 8x8x2-inch pan.

5. Bake at 350°, 35-40 minutes. While hot, cut into squares. Makes 16 brownies.

Julie Metron
STERLING HEIGHTS

Brownies for Kids to Make

4 eggs
2 cups sugar
1 cup butter
4 ounces unsweetened chocolate
1 cup flour
1 package (6 ounces) chocolate chips

Beat eggs and sugar together until thick and light. Melt butter and baking chocolate together; add to egg mixture. Mix in flour.

Pour into 13x9-inch greased and floured pan. Sprinkle chocolate chips over top of batter.

Bake at 350° for 25-30 minutes. Do not overbake.

Brownies will be fudge-like. Cool and cut into squares.

Jennifer & Jackie Vail
BLOOMFIELD HILLS

Chocolate Mint Sticks

(These brownies are always a hit. They are ideal for picnics and pot-lucks, but with a tint of green food coloring added to the mint frosting, pretty enough for a shower or party. They keep best if refrigerated. Sometimes I use melted chocolate chips instead of Baker's chocolate for the glaze–it's cheaper.)

  ½ cup butter
  1 cup sugar
  2 eggs
  1 teaspoon vanilla
  2 ounces unsweetened chocolate, melted
  ½ cup sifted flour
  Pinch of salt
  ½ cup chopped nuts

Cream butter and sugar. Beat in eggs and vanilla. Blend in melted chocolate. Stir in flour, salt and nuts. Pour into greased 8x8x2-inch pan. Bake at 350° for 25 minutes. Cool and spread with frosting and glaze.

Mint Frosting

1 cup sifted confectioners sugar
2 tablespoons soft butter
1 tablespoon milk
1 teaspoon peppermint extract

Combine sugar, butter, milk and peppermint. Beat. Spread over cooled brownie layer. Let stand in refrigerator. Make glaze.

Glaze

2 ounces sweetened chocolate
1 tablespoons butter

Melt chocolate with butter and spread over frosting. Chill until firm. Cut brownies into 1x3-inch sticks.
Keeps best refrigerated.

Cathy House
HARRISON

Bonbon Brownies

(These were always requested at bake sales and P.T.A. meetings when my sons, Chuck and Rich, were in school. Now it is for club gatherings.)

Sift together:
> **⅔ cup flour**
> **¼ cup cocoa**
> **¼ teaspoon salt**
> **½ teaspoon baking powder**

Cream:
> **½ cup shortening**
> **¾ cup sugar**

Add:
> **1 egg**
> **1 egg yolk**
> **1 teaspoon vanilla**
> **¼ cup pecans (chopped)**

Mix ingredients together and spread in a well-greased 8x8x2-inch pan.

Beat:
> **1 egg white**
> **¼ teaspoon cream of tartar**

Add:
> **¼ cup sugar,** and beat until it peaks

Fold in:
> **¼ cup pecans**

Spread on top brownies. Bake 30-35 minutes at 350°. Cut into bars when cold.

(Bars will look like you frosted them.)

Doris Clark Elias
DETROIT

18

Swedish Brownies

1 stick butter or oleo
1 cup sugar*
1 cup flour
2 eggs
½ teaspoon almond extract
½ cup chopped nuts
I have cut down on sugar and only use ¾ cup.

Melt butter in saucepan. Take from burner. Add sugar. When cool add eggs. Fold in flour; add extract and nuts. Bake at 350° 20-25 minutes.

To double recipe, double everything, except use 3 eggs and bake in 9x13-inch pan.

Peggy Bowker
BIRMINGHAM

Kahlua Brownies

1 cup butter
½ cup water
½ cup Kahlua
⅓ cup unsweetened cocoa powder
2 cups all purpose flour
2 cups sugar
1 teaspoon baking soda
½ teaspoon salt
2 slightly beaten eggs
½ cup buttermilk
1½ teaspoon vanilla

In saucepan combine butter, water, Kahlua and cocoa powder. Bring to boiling, stirring constantly. Remove from heat. In large mixing bowl stir together flour, sugar, baking soda and salt; stir in eggs, buttermilk and vanilla. Add cocoa mixture; mix till blended.

Pour mixture into one greased 15½x10½x1-inch baking pan. Bake at 375° 20 minutes. Immediately pour frosting over brownies; spread evenly. Cool; cut into bars. Makes 60 brownies.

Frosting

¼ cup butter
3 tablespoons unsweetened cocoa powder
3 tablespoons Kahlua
2¼ cups sifted powdered sugar
½ cup chopped walnuts
½ teaspoon vanilla

In saucepan combine butter, cocoa powder and Kahlua. Cook till boiling. Beat in sugar, nuts and vanilla.

Janise Mapes
WALLED LAKE

Buddy Brownies

(Named for three wonderful "buddies" of mine.)

Melt together:
>**12 ounces chocolate chip morsels**
>**⅓ cup butter**

Add:
>**2 cups graham cracker crumbs**
>**1 cup chopped nuts**

In another bowl mix together:
>**8 ounces cream cheese**
>**14 ounces sweetened condensed milk**
>**1½ teaspoons vanilla**
>**1 egg**

Press half of crumb mixture in greased 13x9-inch pan. Pour blended ingredients over. Then sprinkle remaining crumb mixture over top.

Bake 25-30 minutes at 350°.

Debbie Jones
STERLING HEIGHTS

21

Rum Raisin Brownies I

(This recipe came from my mother, and has been in the family a long time. I always bake the Rum Raisin Brownies for my family, and when we have company, we love them.)

½ cup raisins
¼ cup dark rum
¼ pound butter
4 ounces unsweetened chocolate
1 ounce semi-sweet chocolate
3 eggs
1¼ cup sugar
1 teaspoon vanilla extract
1 cup flour
¼ teaspoon salt
½ cup coarsely chopped walnuts or pecans

Soak raisins in rum for 20 minutes.

Combine butter and chocolates in top pan of double boiler, and melt over hot water. Stir to blend. Cool slightly.

Beat eggs until thick and lemon-colored. Gradually beat in sugar.

Stir in chocolate and butter mixture, vanilla extract, flour and salt, mixing just until blended.

Mix in nuts, raisins and rum.

Pour into a buttered and floured 9-inch square pan.

Bake at 350° for 25 minutes, or until set but still moist.

Let cool. Cut into squares.

Lena Coppola
SOUTHFIELD

Black Forest Brownies

5 tablespoons butter
3 ounces unsweetened chocolate
1 cup sugar
4 ounces Philadelphia cream cheese
    (½ of 8-ounce package)
¾ cup, plus 2 tablespoons, flour
Pinch of salt
3 eggs
1 teaspoon vanilla
½ cup shelled walnuts (chopped)
1 20-ounce can cherry pie filling

Preheat oven to 350°.
Grease and flour an 8-inch square pan.
Melt butter and chocolate in a bowl over hot water or in a double boiler, then add sugar. Sift the flour and salt in bowl and stir in chocolate mixture, cream cheese, beaten eggs, vanilla and walnuts. Beat until smooth.
Pour into prepared pan. Bake for 25 minutes, then spread cherry pie filling over the brownies. Bake 5-10 minutes more, or until the brownies leave the sides of the pan. Cool slightly before cutting.
Makes 16 squares.

Joyce Rzepa
JACKSON

Peggy's Brownies

(Peggy, who's been making these brownies for more than 40 years, won first prize with these in a baking contest at the hospital where she is employed. At pot lucks, Peggy is always asked to please bring her brownies.)

Melt **4 squares chocolate** with **1 cup shortening.** Add **2 cups sugar** and stir well. Beat **4 eggs** and add to mixture. Add **1 teaspoon vanilla, 1½ cups flour** and **1 teaspoon salt.** Mix well by hand. Do NOT use electric mixer. Add **1 cup chopped nuts.**

Grease a 9x13-inch pan. Bake at 375° for 20 minutes.

Set pan on rack to cool for 5 minutes. Cut into squares.

Peggy Allor
DETROIT

Joann's Best Brownies

(I got this recipe from one of my oldest friends. My family likes it best because it is moist and chocolatey–they love anything chocolate.)

>1 package (4 1/8-ounce size) instant
>   chocolate pudding
>½ cup flour
>¼ teaspoon baking powder
>½ cup butter or margarine
>⅔ cup sugar
>2 eggs
>2 teaspoons vanilla
>½ cup chopped walnuts

Combine pudding, flour, and baking powder in bowl and mix well. Melt butter in saucepan. Remove from heat; add sugar. Beat in eggs, one at a time. Blend in vanilla and pudding mixture. Stir in nuts. Spread in a greased 9-inch square pan. Bake at 350° for 35 minutes. (Check after 25 minutes with toothpick to see if they are done.) Cool in pan. Cut in bars.

Joann Cearloch
FRASER

Virg's Zucchini Brownies

(With the availability of zucchini late in the summer, it was necessary to come up with yet another receipe to utilize this abundant vegetable. I have won a blue ribbon in the Michigan State Fair for this recipe.)

    2 cups flour
    1½ cups sugar
    1 teaspoon salt
    ½ cup cocoa
    1½ teaspoons soda
    2 eggs
    ½ cup chopped nuts
    2 teaspoons vanilla
    2 cups zucchini (peeled and seeded)
    ½ cup vegetable oil

Sift dry ingredients together and combine with rest of ingredients. Spread dough in greased 9x13-inch pan and bake 30 minutes in 350° oven.

Virginia Lee Skrzyniarz
NEW BALTIMORE

~~~~~~Best Brownies (Mocha-Nut)~~~~~~

8 squares unsweetened chocolate
8 ounces (2 sticks) sweet butter
5 eggs (large or extra-large)
1 tablespoon vanilla extract
1 teaspoon almond extract
½ teaspoon salt
2½ tablespoons dry instant espresso or other
    powdered (not granular) coffee
3¾ cups granulated sugar
1⅔ cup sifted all-purpose flour
8 ounces (2 generous cups) walnut halves or large pieces

1. Adjust rack one-third up from bottom of oven. Preheat oven to
425°. Line a 9x19x2-inch pan with foil. Brush the foil with soft or
melted butter.

2. Place the chocolate and the butter in the top of a double boiler
over hot water on moderate heat or in a 4-6 cup heavy saucepan over
low heat. Stir occasionally until the chocolate and butter are melted.
Stir to mix. Remove from heat and set aside.

3. In the large bowl of an electric mixer, beat the eggs with the
vanilla, almond extract, salt, dry instant coffee and sugar at high
speed for 10 minutes. On low speed add the chocolate mixture and
beat only until mixed. Then add the flour and beat only until mixed.
Remove from mixer and stir in the nuts.

4. Turn into prepard pan and smooth the top.

5. Bake 30 to 35 minutes. Check at 30 minutes. If the brownies
seem to be turning quite dark at the edges, remove from oven.
Otherwise continue baking another five minutes. There will be a
thick crust on top and a toothpick inserted in the center will NOT
come out clean.

6. Allow to cool to room temperature. Invert pan onto a rack,
peel off the foil, invert again, and allow to stand 6-8 hours or
overnight before cutting into squares or bars. Wrap individually in
plastic. DO NOT ALLOW TO DRY OUT.

Yield: 32 large brownies.

Jean Schneider-Claytor
ANN ARBOR

Texas Brownies

2 sticks margarine (soft)
2 cups sugar
⅓ cup cocoa
4 eggs
1½ cup flour
1 cup nuts–walnuts or pecans, broken
1 package of miniature marshmallows

Cream margarine, sugar and cocoa. Add eggs, flour and beat well. Stir in nuts. Mixture will be thick. Turn into a 9x13x1-inch cake pan which has been lined with foil and greased. Bake for 30 minutes at 350°.

While hot and in pan, cover brownies with marshmallows. Cover pan with a dish towel to retain heat.

Frosting

1 box sifted confectioners sugar
⅓ cup cocoa
½ stick melted margarine
⅓ cup evaporated milk (or more, if needed)
½ teaspoon vanilla

Mix all ingredients together. (Mixture will be thin.) Drizzle over marshmallows and spread with back of a spoon. Cool 2 hours. Remove foil and eat.

Helen L. Cockerill
TRENTON

Carob Oat Brownies

½ cup butter
1 egg
1 teaspoon vanilla
1 teaspoon orange peel
1 teaspoon lemon peel
1 cup pitted, chopped dates
⅓ cup carob powder
1 cup rolled oats
½ cup pastry flour
½ cup wheat germ
1 teaspoon baking powder
½ teaspoon ground allspice
½ teaspoon nutmeg
½ teaspoon cinnamon
⅔ cup milk

Combine butter and egg; beat well. Add vanilla, orange peel, lemon peel, dates and carob powder; combine thoroughly.

In separate bowl, stir together oats, flour, wheat germ, baking powder and three spices. Combine two mixes; add milk and beat until blended.

Spread batter in a 10x15-inch rimmed baking dish. Sprinkle with **carob chips or nuts**. Bake 25 minutes at 325°.

Yield: about two dozen.

Marcelle Levine
HUNTINGTON WOODS

29

❖❖❖❖❖❖❖❖❖❖❖❖Buttermilk Brownies❖❖❖❖❖❖❖❖❖❖❖❖❖

1 cup margarine
⅓ cup cocoa
1 cup water
2 cups flour
2 cups sugar
1 teaspoon soda
½ teaspoon salt
2 eggs, slightly beaten
½ cup buttermilk
1½ teaspoons vanilla

Bring to boil the margarine, cocoa and water. Combine dry
ingredients; add eggs, buttermilk and vanilla. Blend in cocoa mixture.
Bake in a greased 11x15-inch pan at 375° for 20 minutes. Frost while
hot.

❖❖❖❖❖❖❖❖❖❖❖❖❖❖❖❖❖❖❖❖❖❖❖❖

Frosting

¼ cup margarine
3 tablespoons cocoa
3 tablespoons buttermilk
2½ cups sifted powdered sugar
1 teaspoon vanilla
1 cup chopped walnuts

Bring margarine, cocoa and buttermilk to a boil. Stir in sugar and
vanilla. Fold in nuts.

Virginia Lee Skrzyniarz
New Baltimore

Frosted Raisin-Nut Brownies

(I have been making these brownies for over 25 years. They're always requested when it's our turn to host the 4-H boys and their leaders. Good looking–good tasting. They're a favorite at church bazaars, luncheons and showers, and easily carried to picnics.)

    2 cups lightly packed brown sugar
    4 eggs, well beaten
    1 teaspoon salt
    2 cups flour
    1 teaspoon cinnamon
    1 cup seedless raisins
    ½ cup nuts (optional)

Beat eggs till light and lemon-colored. Gradually add sugar. Continue beating and slowly add salt, flour and cinnamon. Sprinkle a bit of flour over nuts and raisins. Add last.

Spread in well-greased small cookie sheet. Bake 12-15 minutes, until lightly tan. (They should look a bit underdone.)

Cool slightly. Frost quickly with a thin powdered sugar frosting. Use either vanilla, lemon or maple frosting flavoring. Cut into bars.

Ellamae Blackburn
Durand

Almond Brownie Bars

½ cup butter
1 cup ground blanched almonds
⅓ cup granulated sugar
1 cup all-purpose flour
Brownie Layer (recipe follows)
(Almond Paste Layer) recipe follows
½ cup finely chopped unblanched almonds

Mix together butter, the 1 cup ground almonds, sugar and flour. Press mixture gently over bottom of a 9-inch square baking pan.

Gently spread Brownie Layer over the top.

Then top Brownie Layer with Almond Paste Layer.

Sprinkle with ½ cup chopped almonds.

Bake in a preheated 350°-oven 50 minutes, or until sides begin to pull away from pan and center is firm. When cool, cut into 2x1-inch bars.

Makes 32 bars.

Brownie Layer

¼ cup butter
1 square (1 ounce) unsweetened chocolate
⅓ cup granulated sugar
1 egg
¾ cup all-purpose flour

Melt butter and chocolate in saucepan over low heat, stirring often. Cool partially, then beat in sugar, egg and flour.

Almond Paste Layer

1½ cups whole blanched almonds
1½ cups sifted confectioners sugar
1 egg white
1 teaspoon almond extract

Grind the almonds to a fine powder in blender. Beat egg white till soft peaks form; gradually add the confectioners sugar. Add the almond extract. Fold in the fine-ground almonds.

Gently spread over Brownie Layer. Sprinkle with ½ cup chopped almonds.

Bake.

Jean Norris
WEST BLOOMFIELD

Two-Tone Brownies

(This recipe was always a "special" with our sons.)

Layer I

1 cup quick-cooking rolled oats
⅓ cup flour
⅓ cup brown sugar
⅓ cup butter or margarine (melted)

Combine oats, flour, brown sugar and butter–mix well. Press into an 8x8x2-inch pan. Bake in 350° oven 10 minutes.

Layer II

¼ cup shortening
⅔ cup sugar
½ teaspoon vanilla
1 ounce (1 square) unsweetened chocolate, melted
1 egg
⅔ cup flour
1 teaspoon baking powder
Dash salt
⅓ cup milk

Cream shortening and sugar; blend in vanilla and chocolate. Beat in egg. Sift together dry ingredients; add alternately with milk. Spread over first layer. Bake 30 minutes longer. Cool. Cut into squares. Enjoy!

Laura Sadler
Trenton

Molasses Brownies

(This recipe is quick, and uses up leftover graham crackers after the box has been opened awhile.)

1⅓ cups sweetened condensed milk
¼ cup molasses
2 cups graham crackers
1 cup chopped nuts

Heat condensed milk and molasses in a heavy pan; cook over low heat, stirring constantly, for 5 minutes or until mixture thickens.

Remove from heat; add graham cracker crumbs and chopped nuts; mix thoroughly.

Spread the dough evenly in a 6x10-inch pan lined with greased paper. Bake in 350° oven about 15 minutes. Remove from pan immediately; strip off paper and cut in squares. Makes 2 dozen.

Pherne Bobcean
Mt. Clemens

Chocolate-Raspberry Brownies

½ cup sugar
½ cup butter
1 egg
1 envelope Choco-bake pre-melted chocolate
1 cup flour
1 teaspoon baking powder
½ cup raspberry jam
¼ cup butter or margarine
1 egg
1 teaspoon vanilla
1 cup sugar
2 cups coconut

Beat ½ cup sugar, ½ cup butter or margarine and egg well. A chocolate.
Sift together flour and baking powder.
Blend into batter.
Spread batter in an 8x8x2-inch pan.
Cover with raspberry jam.
Melt butter or margarine, and set aside to cool.
Beat egg and vanilla; add sugar.
Blend in cooled butter or margarine and coconut.
Spread over jam.
Bake at 350° for 30 minutes, or until golden.
Cool; cut into 16 squares.

❧❧ Orange Date Brownies ❧❧

(This recipe has been in my family for more than 35 years. I bake it every Christmas and on special holidays. We like its orange, nut and date combination.)

Sift together:
> **1¼ cups flour**
> **¾ teaspoon soda**

Combine in large saucepan:
> **8 ounces cut-up dates**
> **¾ cup brown sugar**
> **½ cup water**
> **½ cup butter**

Cook over low heat, stirring until dates are soft. Remove from heat and stir in **6 ounces semi-sweet chocolate morsels**. Add **2 eggs**, and mix well.

Add dry ingredients with **½ cup orange juice** and **½ cup milk**. Blend thoroughly. Stir in **1 cup walnuts**.

Spread in well-greased 15x10x1-inch jelly roll pan. Bake at 350° for 25-30 minutes.

Cool and frost. Cut in squares.

Orange Glaze

Combine **1½ cups powdered sugar, 2 tablespoons soft butter** and **1 teaspoon grated orange rind**.

Blend in **2-3 tablespoons cream**, until of spreading consistency. Makes three dozen bars.

Barbara D. Kendra
ALLEN PARK

 Amaretto

(This recipe came from a combination of recipes "home tested" with different liquors. It works equally well using Kahlua in place of Amaretto. One reason it's my favorite, besides taste, is the amount it makes and the length of time.

I work as a waitress at T.G.I. Friday's restaurant in Southfield and once or twice a month we are all required to be "shift leader," which means we are in charge of the employees for that day. As such, I bring a "treat" for everyone, which is this recipe. I never make less than 2 pans and then there are always cries of "more.")

2 cups unsifted all-purpose flour
¼ teaspoon salt
6 ounces unsweetened chocolate
½ pound unsalted sweet butter
1 teaspoon vanilla extract
2 tablespoons Saronna Amaretto liquer
2 teaspoons almond extract
2 cups sugar
1 cup firmly packed brown sugar
⅔ cup white corn syrup
6 eggs
3 cups walnut or pecan halves or large pieces

Brownies

Preheat oven to 350°. Grease a 15½x10½x1-inch jelly roll pan. Line it with a piece of waxed paper. Butter the paper and dust very lightly with flour. Set aside.

Measure flour before sifting; sift together with salt and set aside. Melt chocolate in the top of a double boiler over medium heat. Stir until smooth and remove from heat.

In the large bowl of an electric mixer, cream the butter. Add vanilla, almond extract, Amaretto and both sugars, beating to mix well. Add corn syrup and beat until smooth. Add eggs one at a time, beating until smooth after each addition. Beat in melted chocolate just until mixed.

On low speed, gradually add flour mixture, scraping bowl with spatula as necessary and mix until smooth. Stir in 2 cups of the nuts by hand–you will have 1 cup left.

Turn the mixture into the prepared pan and spread to make a smooth layer. The pan will be filled to the top. Sprinkle the remaining nuts evenly over the top.

Bake for 35 minutes–no more. Remove from oven and let cool for 30 minutes. Cover with a large rack or cookie sheet and invert. Remove the pan and the waxed paper. Cover again with pan and invert, leaving right side up. Let them cool completely.

Use a serrated or sharp thin knife to cut into squares. Wrap each individually or store in air-tight container. Excellent frosted with a commercially prepared chocolate frosting or left unfrosted.

Makes 32 large brownies.

Josephine A. Costew
FERNDALE

Polka Dot Brownies

½ cup shortening (Crisco, Spry)
2 squares unsweetened chocolate (2 ounces)
¾ cup sifted flour
½ teaspoon baking powder
½ teaspoon salt
2 eggs
1 cup sugar
1 teaspoon vanilla
½ cup nuts, cut up
½ cup miniature marshmallows

Melt shortening and chocolate together over hot water. Cool.
Sift flour with baking powder and salt. Beat eggs in large bowl until light. Add sugar, then add the chocolate mixture. Blend.
Add flour, vanilla, nuts and marshmallows.
Mix well. Bake in greased 8x8x2-inch pan at 350° for 30-35 minutes.

Elizabeth Kurk
Mt. Clemens

MSU Brownies

(Ever heard of chocolate cheese? Well, these brownies, like chocolate cheese, are not for everyone. As my mother says, "I like chocolate and I like cheese, but not together."

But, back to the brownies. These contain chocolate cheese, a sort of rubbery version of fudge invented at Michigan State University some time ago. It used to be that the only place you could buy this stuff was at the MSU Dairy. However, I recently purchased some at Kroger's so it does seem to have widened its market.

While a student at MSU I never actually ate brownies with chocolate cheese in them–not that I ever knew of anyway. But while experimenting in my kitchen one day with chocolate cheese–the possibilities are either very limited or endless depending on your outlook–I came up with these. While no one confessed to liking them a whole lot, nonetheless they were gone within a day. So, bake at your own risk–eat at your own peril.

2 squares (2 ounces) unsweetened chocolate
1 cup flour
½ teaspoon baking powder
½ teaspoon salt
½ cup butter or margarine
½ teaspoon vanilla
1 cup sugar
2 eggs
1 cup walnuts
1 cup coarsely chopped chocolate cheese

Melt chocolate and set aside.
Sift together flour, baking powder and salt. Set aside.
Cream butter, vanilla and sugar. Beat in eggs.
Add chocolate to mixture, blending well.
Mix in dry ingredients until well blended.
Stir in walnuts and chocolate cheese.
Spread in greased 9x9-inch pan. Bake at 350° 40-45 minutes.
Cool in pan. Cut into squares.
Makes about 16 brownies.

41

Fudge Nut Brownies

1 cup butter or oleo
2 cups light brown sugar
2 eggs
2 teaspoons vanilla
2½ cups sifted flour
1 teaspoon baking soda
1 teaspoon salt
3 cups quick oats, uncooked

Cream butter and sugar; mix in eggs and vanilla. Sift together flour, soda and salt; add to rolled oats. Stir into creamed mixture and set aside.

Fudge Nut Filling:

1 12-ounce package semi-sweet chocolate pieces
1 cup Eagle Brand sweetened condensed milk
2 tablespoons butter or oleo
½ teaspoon salt
1 cup chopped nuts
1 teaspoon vanilla

In a saucepan over boiling water, mix together chocolate pieces, sweetened condensed milk, butter and salt. Stir until smooth. Stir in nuts and vanilla.

Spread about ⅔ of oatmeal mixture in a greased 9x13-inch pan. Cover with chocolate mixture. Dot with remaining oatmeal mixture. Bake at 350° for 25-30 minutes or until lightly browned.

Catherine Endicott
MIDLAND

Cherry Bright Brownies

(This recipe was printed in the Orlando (Florida) Sentinal *paper about 10 years ago. I prepared the brownies more out of curiosity than anything else and, needless to say, they became one of my family's favorites.)*

⅓ cup butter or margarine
¾ cup sugar
2 eggs
¼ cup light corn syrup
2 tablespoons kirsch (or other cherry liqueur or 1 teaspoon almond extract)
1 teaspoon vanilla
⅔ cup all-purpose flour
⅓ cup cocoa
½ teaspoon salt
¼ teaspoon baking powder
½ cup chopped, well-drained maraschino cherries
⅓ cup slivered almonds

Cream butter, sugar and eggs; blend in corn syrup, kirsch and vanilla. Add flour, cocoa, salt and baking powder; blend until combined.

Stir in cherries and almonds. Pour into greased and floured 9-inch square pan. Bake at 350° for 25-30 minutes or until brownies begin to pull away from pan.

Frost, if desired, and garnish with additional cherries.

Martha M. White
NATIONAL CITY

Butterscotch Brownies I

(This recipe is from a cookbook containing healthful recipes, and that's why it's so popular with me. It's nutritious and low-cal, and best of all, everyone who's tried it loves it! I feel good about serving it–it's not "junk" or "empty calories.")

Preheat oven to 350°.
Melt:
> ¼ cup margarine

Add:
> 1 tablespoon dark molasses
> ¾ cup sugar
> 2 eggs, beaten
> 2 teaspoons vanilla

Stir well.
Sift in:
> ½ cup, plus 2 tablespoons instant nonfat dry milk
> ½ teaspoon baking powder
> 1/8 teaspoon salt

Add:
> 1 cup wheat germ
> ½ cup walnuts or pecans, finely chopped (I use pecans)

Stir only enough to blend, using no more than 25 strokes. Spread in greased 8x8-inch pan. Bake 30 minutes.

Vicki J. Stewart
GRAND RAPIDS

Butterscotch Brownies II

Melt:
   4 tablespoons butter or oleo
Add:
   1 cup brown sugar
   1 beaten egg
   1 cup flour, sifted
   1 teaspoon baking powder

Mix and add **dash of salt**. Add **1 teaspoon vanilla** and **¼ cup nutmeats** (optional).
Bake at 325° for 20-25 minutes in a glass pie dish.

Laverne Koetsier
GRAND HAVEN

Brownie Miniatures

Nut Crust:
3 tablespoons butter or margarine
3 tablespoons sugar
¾ cup finely chopped walnuts

Blend butter with sugar and chopped nuts. Line 9-inch square pan with foil and press nut mixture over bottom of pan.

Brownie Filling:
½ cup butter or margarine, softened
1 cup sugar
3 eggs
2 squares (2 ounces) unsweetened chocolate, melted
1 teaspoon vanilla
⅓ cup all purpose flour, sifted
½ teaspoon baking powder
1/8 teaspoon salt

Place all ingredients in mixing bowl. Mix at low speed or by hand until smooth.
Turn into nut-lined pan and bake at 325° 35-40 minutes. Cool.

Chocolate Glaze:
½ cup semi-sweet chocolate chips
2 tablespoons butter or margarine

Melt chocolate; add butter and stir until smooth. Pour over cooled brownies.
Put in refrigerator to cool. Cut into mini-pieces.

Gerrie Bethke
MT. CLEMENS

Lemon Brownies

1 cup, plus 2 tablespoons flour
½ cup butter (not margarine)
¼ cup powdered sugar
2 eggs, slightly beaten
1 cup granulated sugar
¼ teaspoon salt
3 tablespoons lemon juice
½ teaspoon baking powder

Cream 1 cup flour, butter and powdered sugar. Press into an 8-inch square pan. Bake 20 minutes at 350°. Cool

Mix eggs, granulated sugar, salt and lemon juice. Add remaining flour and baking powder. Pour on top of baked crust and bake for 25 more minutes.

Remove from oven and sprinkle with **powdered sugar** immediately. Cool thoroughly before cutting into squares.

(These are so buttery, they are sinful.)

Michelle DeLand-Duffy
WARREN

Brown Sugar Brownies

2 eggs
1⅓ cups packed brown sugar
3 tablespoons butter or margarine
1 cup flour
1 teaspoon baking powder
1 teaspoon ginger
¼ teaspoon salt
1 cup chopped nuts

Beat eggs in top part of double boiler. Stir in sugar and cook over boiling water, stirring constantly until sugar is dissolved–about 10 minutes.

Remove from heat and stir in butter or margarine.

Sift together flour, baking powder, ginger and salt. Add to cooked mixture, thoroughly mixing. Stir in the chopped nuts.

Bake at 300° for 35 minutes in an 8x8-inch baking pan.

Cool. Cut into squares.

Makes 20.

Cottage Cheese Brownies

(Favorite of the staff of the United States Pavilion at the 1982 World's Fair in Knoxville, Tennessee and the U.S. Department of Commerce in Detroit. Old southern recipe. They're moist and chewy; just great!)

3 squares unsweetened chocolate
½ cup butter
1¼ cups sugar
1½ teaspoons vanilla
1 tablespoon cornstarch
¾ cup creamed cottage cheese
3 eggs
½ teaspoon lemon juice
½ cup unsifted all-purpose flour
½ teaspoon baking powder
¼ teaspoon salt
½ cup chopped walnuts
½ teaspoon almond extract

Preheat oven to 350°.

Melt chocolate and 6 tablespoons butter over hot water.

Cream remaining 2 tablespoons butter, ¼ cup sugar and ½ teaspoon vanilla. Add cornstarch, cottage cheese, 1 egg and lemon juice; beat till smooth. Set aside

Beat remaining 2 eggs till thick. With spoon, stir in remaining 1 cup sugar. Beat with spoon till mixed. Stir in chocolate mixture.

Mix and sift together flour, baking powder and salt. Stir into chocolate mixture. Mix in nuts, remaining 1 teaspoon vanilla and almond extract.

Spoon ½ batter into greased 9-inch square pan. Cover with cottage cheese mixture, and then rest of batter. Bake for 35 minutes, or till top springs up under slight pressue.

Mara Yachnin
FARMINGTOM HILLS

49

Three Layer Brownies

Bottom Layer:

½ cup flour
¼ teaspoon baking soda
¼ teaspoon salt
1 cup rolled oats
½ cup brown sugar
6 tablespoons butter, melted

Sift together dry ingredients. Mix with rolled oats and sugar. Melt butter in 8x8x2-inch baking pan. Mix dry ingredients with butter in pan. Pat mixture down to the bottom of pan. Bake at 350° for 10 minutes.

Middle Layer:

1 ounce (1 square) unsweetened chocolate
4 tablespoons butter
¾ cup sugar
1 egg
⅔ cup flour & ½ teaspoon baking powder
¼ teaspoon salt
¼ cup milk
½ teaspoon vanilla
½ cup chopped nuts

Melt chocolate and butter in a heavy saucepan over low heat. Remove from heat and combine with sugar. Add the egg and beat well. Sift together the four, baking powder and salt. Add alternatingly with milk and vanilla. Fold in nuts and spread batter over bottom layer. Bake at 350° for 25 minutes.

Top Layer:

1 ounce (1 square) unsweetened chocolate
2 tablespoons butter
1½ cups confectioners sugar
1 teaspoon vanilla
2-3 tablespoons hot water

Melt chocolate and butter in a small saucepan over low heat. Remove from heat–add confectioners sugar and vanilla. Blend in enough hot water to make pouring consistency. Spread over cooled brownies. Cut into small rectangles.

Margaret A. Lefkowitz
MT. CLEMENS

Jessica's Favorite
Snickers Brownies

(Fantastico. But don't overbake these or you'll end up with Snickers burned to the bottom of the pan.)

1 box brownie mix (enough for 8x8-inch pan)
2 2-ounce Snickers candy bars

Make brownie batter according to package directions.
Cut up candy bars into small pieces. Separate into two piles.
Fold one pile of Snickers into batter.
Spread in prepared 8x8-inch pan and bake.
Five minutes before taking from oven, sprinkle second pile of Snickers over top of brownies.
When done, spread melted Snickers over top of brownies with the back of a spoon–don't worry if it clumps-up; it's the taste that counts.
Cool. Cut in squares.
If you make a 9x13-inch batch, just double up on the Snickers.

~~~~~~Harold's Favorite Brownies~~~~~~

(The maple sugar lends a very subtle, complimentary flavor to the chocolate. As a change, I will often substitute carob chips in place of chocolate ones.)

1 cup maple sugar*
2 eggs (at room temperature)
⅓ cup softened butter
2 ounces chocolate, unsweetened
1 teaspoon vanilla extract
⅔ cup unsifted whole wheat flour
½ teaspoon baking powder
¼ teaspoon salt
½ cup chopped nuts
¼ cup large chocolate chips (semi-sweet)

Maple syrup granules (maple sugar) can be purchased at the Nutri Foods Health Food Store located on Main Street in Royal Oak.

In bowl, combine maple sugar, eggs, butter, chocolate (the 2 ounces) and vanilla; beat until creamy. Add flour, baking powder and salt; mix well. Mix in nuts and chocolate chips. Spread batter in an 8-inch square, greased baking pan.

Bake at 350° for 25-35 minutes. Cool completely and cut into 2-inch squares.

Yield: 16 2-inch squares.

Nadyne Linton
SOUTHFIELD

Choco-Banana Brownies
(They stay moist and fresh. They're also very nourishing.)

1 cup semi-sweet chocolate chips
1 cup sifted flour
½ teaspoon baking powder
¼ teaspoon baking soda
1 teaspoon salt
½ teaspoon cinnamon
¼ cup soft margarine or butter
¾ cup sugar
1 cup mashed ripe bananas
1 egg
¼ cup milk
1 cup all bran
1 cup nut meats (optional)

Method:
1. Melt chocolate over hot water. Cool.
2. Sift dry ingredients, through cinnamon.
3. Combine butter, sugar, bananas, egg, milk, all bran, and chocolate. Beat until well-blended.
4. Add dry ingredients and nut meats. Beat until well combined.
5. Spread in greased, floured 9x13-inch pan. Bake in 350° oven for 25 minutes.

Chocolate Velvet Frosting

1 cup chocolate chips
2 tablespoons shortening
1 cup sifted icing sugar
¼ cup milk
1/8 teaspoon salt
¼ teaspoon vanilla

Method:
1. Melt chocolate and shortening over hot (not boiling) water. Remove from heat.
2. Add remaining ingredients and beat until smooth.
3. Spread frosting over cooled brownies.

Mrs. A. Borschke
MIDLAND

Austrian Chocolate Squares

½ cup butter
½ cup brown sugar
1 egg yolk
1 cup coarsely chopped semi-sweet chocolate
½ teaspoon lemon rind
1 teaspoon vanilla
¼ cup water
1 cup flour
1 egg white

Cream together the butter and sugar. Add egg yolk and beat well.
Beat in the chocolate, lemon rind, vanilla and water.
Stir in the flour.
Beat egg white until stiff; fold into chocolate mixture.
Bake at 375° for 30 minutes in an 8x8-inch greased pan.
Cool. Cut into squares. Sprinkle with **powdered sugar.**

Apricot-Chocolate Brownies

¾ cup dried apricots
2 ounces unsweetened chocolate
¾ cup flour
¼ teaspoon baking soda
¼ teaspoon baking powder
¼ teaspoon salt
½ cup (1 stick) butter or margarine
1 cup sugar
2 eggs

Soak apricots in warm water about 1 hour. Cut into small chunks.

Melt chocolate over hot water.

Sift together flour, baking soda, baking powder and salt.

Cream butter and sugar together until light and fluffy. Add eggs, beating well.

Gradually add in dry, sifted ingredients. Stir in apricots.

Spread in greased 9x9-inch pan and bake at 350° for 30-40 minutes.

Cool and cut into squares.

May be dusted with powdered sugar, if desired.

True Love Brownies

For over 10 years this recipe's been in the making,
And from the look of my kitchen, you can tell I've been baking.
Having had my share of baking failures, I must confess,
Regrets become lessons of learning as clouds of powdered sugar and
*   smoke subside on my mess.*
Finally, credit belongs to my kids who lick each bowl throughout;
Because even when my loyal brownie testers had their doubts,
Have had to chew and spit dough out,
Here's the result: the "True Love Brownie" made with true
*   love–without a pout.*

1 1/8 cups soft butter, divided
2 cups sugar
3 eggs
1 teaspoon vanilla
2 ounces unsweetened chocolate
6 tablespoons cocoa
1 cup flour
¼ teaspoon salt
1 cup chopped pecans
24 pecan halves
Confectioners sugar

Cream ½ cup butter with granulated sugar. Add eggs and beat until light. Add vanilla; mix. Melt remaining butter with chocolate and cocoa; cool, and beat into first mixture. Add flour, salt and chopped pecans. Mix well and pour into greased and floured 9x13-inch pan. Bake at 350° for about 45 minutes. Cool.

Sift confectioners sugar over top of brownies. Arrange pecan halves on top. Cut into 24 bars.

Rose Adams
DETROIT

Cream Cheese Brownies Supreme

(This recipe was put together solely for the brownie contest and only made once. My friends who were taste testers liked it so well we didn't experiment any further. They all agreed that the recipe should be submitted the way it was.)

Cream Cheese Brownies:

8 ounces German sweet chocolate
10 tablespoons butter
8 ounces cream cheese
2 cups sugar
6 eggs
1 cup, plus 2 tablespoons unsifted flour
1 teaspoon baking powder
½ teaspoon salt
3 teaspoons vanilla
½ teaspoon almond extract
1 cup chopped nuts

Preheat oven to 350°. Grease a 9x13-inch pan.

Melt chocolate and 6 tablespoons butter over very low heat, stirring constantly. Cool.

Cream remaining butter with cream cheese until softened. Gradually add sugar, creaming until light and fluffy. Add eggs one at a time, blending after each addition.

Add flour, baking powder and salt. Blend well. Add melted chocolate, vanilla and almond extract. Stir in nuts.

Set aside.

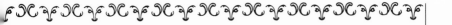

Filling:

8 ounces almond paste
2 eggs
½ cup sugar
1 cup coconut
1 cup mini chocolate chips
1 cup chopped nuts

Blend almond paste, eggs and sugar until smooth. Stir in coconut, mini chocolate chips and nuts.

Pour half of brownie batter into greased pan. Spread filling evenly in pan; pour remaining brownie batter on top completely covering the filling.

Bake 45-50 minutes at 350°.

(Very moist and rich.)

J.M. *Dominowski*
LINWOOD

Homemade Brownie Mix

(This recipe is a great time-saver and money-saver. Having the dry ingredients mixed ahead saves time and it will make enough for several batches of brownies.)

Brownie Mix

4 cups flour
4½ cups sugar
1 cup baking cocoa
1½ cups nonfat dry milk
1½ tablespoons baking powder
1½ teaspoons salt

Sift together and store in airtight container.

To Make Brownies:

1¾ cups mix
1 egg
¼ cup warm water
¼ cup cooking oil
1 teaspoon vanilla
¼ cup chopped nuts
1 cup chocolate chips

Combine mix and liquids. Beat 1 minute at medium speed. Stir in nuts and chips.

Pour into greased 9-inch square pan. Bake at 350° for 30 minutes. For variety, stir in ½ cup peanut butter.

Mary A. Boot
ROYAL OAK

Bangor Brownies

(This recipe is from the Metropolitan Cook Book, published about 1930. Dad loved it.)

¼ cup melted shortening
⅓ cup molasses
1 egg
2 squares melted bitter chocolate
1 cup flour
1 teaspoon baking powder
Few grains salt
1 cup nuts

Sift flour, baking powder and salt together. Mix the ingredients in order given and beat thoroughly.

Spread the mixture evenly on a cake pan that has been lined with oiled paper. Bake 15 minutes in slow oven–325°. Remove the paper from cake as soon as it is taken from oven, and cut into small squares or strips with a sharp knife.

Wanda Peters
Union Lake

Pecan-Date Brownies

1 cup chopped pecans
1 6-ounce package (1 cup) semisweet chocolate chips
¾ cup sifted flour
6 tablespoons cocoa
¼ teaspoon salt
½ cup butter or margarine
1 teaspoon vanilla
1 cup granulated sugar
3 eggs
½ cup ground dates
⅓ cup butter or margarine, softened
1 cup firmly packed brown sugar
1 cup sifted flour
½ teaspoon baking powder
½ teaspoon baking soda
¼ teaspoon salt
1 egg
1 teaspoon vanilla

Mix pecans with the chocolate chips. Set aside.

Sift together the ¾ cup flour, cocoa and ¼ teaspoon salt. Set aside.

Cream ½ cup butter or margarine and 1 teaspoon vanilla; blend in granulated sugar until fluffy. Beat in 3 eggs.

Add dry ingredients, mixing well. Stir in ground dates.

Spread batter in 2 9x9x2-inch pans.

Sprinkle each top with half the pecan mixture.

Set aside.

Cream ⅓ cup butter or margarine and brown sugar. Add the egg and vanilla, beating thoroughly.

Sift together the dry ingredients. Blend into butter mixture.

Spread mixture over batter in two pans.

Bake at 350° about 30 minutes, or until toothpick inserted comes out clean.

Cool slightly; cut into 4 dozen bars.

Orange-Chocolate Brownies

2 1-ounce squares unsweetened chocolate
½ cup (1 stick) butter or margarine
2 eggs
1 cup granulated sugar
1 teaspoon vanilla
½ teaspoon grated orange rind
½ cup sifted flour
1/8 teaspoon salt
1 cup chopped walnuts
½ cup semi-sweet chocolate pieces

Melt chocolate squares and butter or margarine in small saucepan. Remove from heat.

Beat eggs until thick and lemon-colored in medium size bowl; gradually beat in sugar until thick and fluffy. Stir in melted butter and chocolate mixture, vanilla and orange rind.

Blend in flour and salt. Fold in walnuts and semi-sweet chocolate pieces.

Pour into buttered 8x8x2-inch pan. Bake in 350°-oven for 30 minutes, or until a shiny top crust forms. Do not overbake for centers should be fudgelike.

Cool completely in pan on wire cake rack. Loosen around the edges. With a sharp knife, cut into 16 squares. Remove from pan.

Margaret Huntington
BLOOMFIELD HILLS

Peanut Butter Chip Brownies

(Knowing all my children love Reese's peanut butter cups, I thought the peanut butter chips would be ideal combined with my regular brownie recipe. It was an instant hit, and now that's the only way I make my brownies.)

      1⅓ cups flour
      1 teaspoon baking powder
      ½ teaspoon salt
      ⅔ stick oleo
      4 squares Hershey's chocolate
      2 cups sugar
      4 eggs (beaten)
      6 ounces (½ bag) Reese's peanut butter chips

Melt oleo in saucepan with chocolate squares. Set aside to cool. Meanwhile mix or sift dry ingredients together.

Beat eggs; then add sugar gradually to eggs. Continue beating until mixture is smooth.

Add cooled chocolate mixture to egg/sugar combination. Now add dry ingredients. Add vanilla.

Now add the peanut butter chips. I stir them in by hand.

Bake at 350° for 35 minutes.

Dixie Kibler
DETROIT

Marble Brownies

Cream together:
  ½ **cup butter or margarine**
  ¾ **cup granulated sugar**
  1½ **teaspoons vanilla**
Add:
  2 eggs
Beat until blended.
Sift together:
  ⅔ **cup flour**
  ½ **teaspoon baking powder**
  ¼ **teaspoon salt**
Stir into creamed mixture.

Place half the batter in another bowl. Blend in one **1-ounce square unsweetened melted chocolate.** Add ½ **cup nuts** if you desire.

Marble batters in greased 8x8x2-inch pan. (After alternating batters side-by-side in pan, take rubber spatula through the two batters, being careful not to blend too well.)

Bake at 350° for 30 minutes. Cool.

Frosting

2 tablespoons butter or margarine
1 square melted chocolate
1 tablespoon cream
1 tablespoon vanilla
Confectioners sugar

Mix and spread on brownies.

Barb Johnston
DEARBORN HEIGHTS

Blonde Brownies I

2 cups unsifted flour
¼ teaspoon baking soda
1 teaspoon baking powder
½ teaspoon salt
2 cups firmly packed brown sugar
⅔ cups melted shortening or margarine
2 slightly beaten eggs
2 teaspoons vanilla
1 cup or 6-ounce package chocolate chips
⅓ cup chopped nuts

Mix the flour, soda, baking powder and salt; set aside. Add the sugar to the shortening and mix well. Blend in the eggs and vanilla. Gradually add flour mixture. Mix well and spread in a 13x9-inch pan. Sprinkle the chocolate chips and nuts on top. Bake at 350° for 30 minutes. Cool in pan. Cut into squares.

Mrs. Bette Semig
FRASER

Blonde Brownies II

1½ cups sifted flour
2 teaspoons baking powder
½ teaspoon salt
½ cup butter or margarine
1 cup granulated sugar
½ cup (packed) brown sugar
2 eggs
1 teaspoon vanilla
1 bag Heath Brickle

Sift flour, baking powder and salt together.
Cream butter or margarine. Add both sugars and cream well.
Add eggs and vanilla; beat until fluffy.
Blend in dry ingredients.
Stir in Heath Brickle.
Spread over bottom of well-greased 9x13-inch pan.
Bake at 350° for 30 minutes.
If desired, brownies may be frosted (white).
Cut when cool.

Bonnie Schipper
ALMA

Moist and Chewy Heartland Brownies

¾ cup soft butter or margarine
2 cups sugar
3 eggs
1 teaspoon vanilla
3 ounces unsweetened chocolate (melted)
1 tablespoon milk
1 cup sifted all-purpose flour
1 teaspoon baking powder
½ teaspoon salt
1½ cups Heartland Natural Cereal, plain variety

1. Cream butter and sugar until fluffy.
2. Beat in eggs, vanilla, chocolate and milk.
3. Sift together flour, baking powder and salt. Stir in cereal.
4. Spread evenly into greased 13x9x2-inch pan. Bake in 325°
oven for 40-45 minutes, or until center is set. Cut into 36 pieces.

Mrs. R.W. LeMoyne
BIRMINGHAM

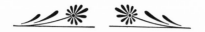

Honey Bear Brownies

(This recipe was passed onto me by a young woman I met while working in Tallahassee, Florida. She was an "Air Force Brat" whose family lived at a base close by. Since they had travelled all over the world while she was growing up, this recipe could have come from anywhere. The one thing we had in common, however, was our love of chocolate. I think these brownies are the best because they're so chewy and crunchy, rather than cakey. Sometimes I even double the amount of nuts that are called for!)

⅓ cup butter or margarine
⅔ cup sugar
½ cup honey (or ¼ cup light corn syrup)
2 teaspoons vanilla
2 eggs (room temperature)
½ cup all-purpose flour
⅓ cup Hershey's cocoa (unsweetened)
½ teaspoon salt
1½ cups chopped walnuts

Cream butter and sugar in a bowl. Blend in honey and vanilla. Add eggs, one at a time, beating well after each addition. Combine flour, cocoa, and salt. Gradually add to creamed mixture. Stir in nuts.

Pour into greased 9x9x1¾-inch baking pan. Bake at 350° for 30-35 minutes or until brownies begin to pull away from edge of pan. Cool. Frost, if desired.

Mary Jean Fitzgibbons
DETROIT

Best Ever Brownies

4 ounces Baker's chocolate (bittersweet) or
 ½ cup Hershey's Cocoa
½ stick butter or margarine
2 cups sugar
4 eggs
2½ cups Bisquick
1 cup nuts (walnuts or pecans)

Melt chocolate and butter together. In large bowl mix sugar, eggs and Bisquick. Add chocolate mixture and nuts. Stir. If too thick add a little water.

Spread in 9x13-inch greased pan. Bake at 350° for 30-35 minutes. Do not overcook.

Icing:

Bring to a boil:

1 stick oleo
6 tablespoons milk
1 teaspoon vanilla

Add:

½ cup nuts (optional)
4 tablespoons cocoa
3½ cups powdered sugar

Spread icing on warm brownies. Let cool, and enjoy.

Darlene L. Kotcher
TROY

Absolutely Foolproof Brownies

(I cut this out of the newspaper years ago–it appealed to me because it was foolproof. So many recipes don't always turn out well. This one does.)

1 12-ounce package semisweet chocolate chips
⅔ cup butter
4 eggs
1 cup sugar
1 cup sifted flour
1 teaspoon baking powder
½ teaspoon salt
2 teaspoons vanilla
Confectioners sugar

Melt chocolate chips and butter over low heat. Beat eggs and sugar until thick. Sift together the sifted flour, baking powder and salt. Add to egg and sugar mixture. Add chocolate mixture and vanilla.

Pour into greased pan 7½x11¾ inches. Bake for 25 minutes at 350°. When cool, sprinkle with confectioners sugar through a sieve.

Joan E. Smith
DETROIT

Mom's Saucepan Brownies

(To tell you how well we like this recipe, let me say that my mom used to make a triple batch everytime she baked these brownies. With five kids, they didn't last too long!!)

> 1 stick margarine
> 2 1-ounce squares unsweetened chocolate
> 1 cup sugar
> 1 cup broken pecans (or walnuts)
> ½ cup flour
> 1 teaspoon baking powder
> 1 teaspoon vanilla
> 2 eggs

Rub bottom of 9x9-inch pan with margarine.

Melt margarine and chocolate in a saucepan (3-quart). Remove from heat. Add all ingredients, except eggs. Mix to blend with spoon. Add eggs and beat well.

Pour into prepared pan and bake in moderate oven (350°) for 30 minutes. Be careful not to burn. Cool. Cut into squares.

Mrs. Kathy Ancona
Detroit

Two-Layer Brownies

1⅓ cup sifted flour
⅓ cup dry bread crumbs
⅓ cup brown sugar
¾ cup nuts, chopped
⅓ cup butter, melted

Blend flour, bread crumbs, brown sugar and nuts. Mix in the melted butter. Press firmly into lightly greased 8-inch square pan and bake at 425° for 5 minutes. Remove from oven and reduce temperature to 350°.

2 eggs, beaten well
½ cup butter, melted
¾ cup brown sugar
2 teaspoons vanilla
¾ cup flour
⅓ cup cocoa
1 teaspoon baking powder
½ teaspoon salt

Combine eggs, butter, brown sugar and vanilla. Sift dry ingredients together. Blend sifted ingredients into egg mixture, mixing well. Pour over baked layer in pan. Return to oven and continue baking at 350° 40-45 minutes. Cool slightly and cut into squares.
Makes 16 squares.

Mary Ann Alverson
OSCODA

Aloha Brownies

(This recipe grew out of a search for a bar cookie using pineapple. While searching through my cookbooks and clippings, I found a recipe for pineapple brownies. When making them, I thought to myself why not add oriental seasoning? If it tasted good added to mayonnaise cake, it should taste great in this. The recipe called for chopped nuts. To make it more exotic I chose to use macadamia nuts and chocolate glaze sprinkled with coconut. As soon as I placed these on the table, my girlfriends and kids saw the brownies...and they were gone–faster than you can strike a match on a wet rock.)

Melt together over hot water:
2 squares unsweetened chocolate

Beat in:
**½ cup Mazola oil
1 cup sugar
2 eggs
1 cup crushed pineapple, well drained
½ teaspoon vanilla
1 cup sifted flour
1½ teaspoons oriental seasoning
(A blend of anise, cinnamon, nutmeg, ginger and cloves)**

Sift together and stir in:
**½ teaspoon baking powder
¼ teaspoon salt
¼ teaspoon baking soda**

Mix in:
½ cup macadamia nuts

Spread in well-greased 8-inch square pan. Bake in moderate oven (350°) 35 to 40 minutes. Cool slightly; top with Chocolate Glaze.

Cool; cut into 16 2-inch squares.

(Use chopped blanched almonds in place of macadamia nuts if not available.)

Chocolate Glaze

Combine **⅔ cup sugar, 3 tablespoons milk** and **3 tablespoons margarine.** Bring to boiling; boil for 30 seconds. Remove from heat; stir in **½ cup semi-sweet chocolate chips** till melted (mixture will be thin). Immediately pour atop brownies; sprinkle **1 cup flaked coconut** on top.

Gwendolyn L. Sherrill
DETROIT

Mom's Super-Moist Brownies

1 stick (½ cup) butter
1 cup sugar
4 eggs
1 teaspoon vanilla
1 cup flour
½ teaspoon salt
1 can (16-ounce size) Hershey's chocolate syrup

Cream butter and sugar until light. Add eggs one at a time. Add syrup, vanilla, flour and salt.

Pour into a greased 9x13-inch pan. Bake at 350° for 25 minutes. Frost.

Frosting:

1 cup sugar
¼ cup milk
2 tablespoons butter
3 ounces semi-sweet chocolate chips
3 ounces butterscotch chips

Bring milk, butter and sugar to full boil over medium heat in saucepan. Stir in chips until melted. Pour over hot brownies; spread quickly as frosting hardens.

Rosemarie Dykstra
GRAND RAPIDS

Orange-Coconut Brownies

½ cup butter
1 squares (2 ounces) unsweetened chocolate
1 cup sugar
2 eggs
2 level tablespoons frozen orange juice
  concentrate, thawed but undiluted
2 teaspoons grated orange peel
⅔ cup flour
¼ teaspoon salt
¼ teaspoon soda
½ cup flaked coconut

In medium-size pan, melt butter and chocolate, stirring constantly; remove from heat. Stir in sugar. Beat in eggs, concentrate and orange peel.

Stir in flour, salt and soda just until blended. Stir in coconut. Turn into a greased 8-inch square pan. Bake in preheated 350°-oven 35 minutes or until toothpick inserted in center comes out clean. Cool in pan on rack. Cut in 2-inch squares.

Makes 16.

Mary Ann Piotrowski
FERNDALE

⟡ Clara's Spicy Brownies ⟡

(This recipe is a variation of an Italian pepper cookie that has been made by the Lello family–my mother's family– for a great many years. As a child I always enjoyed the "different" taste of these cookies, the gentle spicy bite that made your mouth tingle. It would not be Christmas without pepper cookies.)

2 eggs
½ cup sweet butter
⅔ cup sifted flour
⅔ cup chopped, salted cashews
⅔ cup raisins (or chopped dates)
2 squares Baker's chocolate
   (6 tablespoons cocoa substitute, if you must)
1 teaspoon vanilla
1 cup sugar
½ teaspoon of each spice: cloves
   allspice, cinnamon (ground)
¼ teaspoon black pepper
¼ teaspoon cayenne pepper, ground

(Note: A ¼ teaspoons of salt can be added if not using salted nuts or if you feel salt is needed–I do not.)
(Additional note: If using cocoa, add with dry ingredients.)

Cream butter and sugar until light and fluffy. Add eggs, one at a time. Sift flour and salt once. Add dry spices to flour and salt, then add to creamed mixture. Add vanilla, melted chocolate and nuts. Pour into a 9-inch square pan.

Do not bake for more than 25 minutes at 325°. Know your oven and adjust temperature accordingly.

Cool. Cut into squares. If possible, store overnight in airtight tin–the moistness and flavor improves.

Clara Scavo Pare
FARMINGTON

ℑℭ☙Coconut-Cream Filled Brownies☙ℑℭ

½ cup butter
1¼ cup sugar
1 cup flour
⅓ cup cocoa
½ teaspoon baking powder
½ teaspoon salt
3 eggs
1 teaspoon vanilla
1 cup nuts

Grease and flour bottom of 9-inch square pan.
Sift dry ingredients.
Melt butter and stir in sugar. Cool to lukewarm. Blend in eggs one at a time, beating well after each one. Add dry ingredients. Stir in vanilla and nuts.
Bake 30-35 minutes. Cool 10 minutes. Remove from pan and cool completely.

Filling:

1 cup flaked coconut
1 egg
½ cup evaporated milk
¼ cup butter
1 cup firmly packed brown sugar
1 tablespoon flour
1/8 teaspoon salt
1 teaspoon vanilla

Toast coconut in oven at 350° for 10-12 minutes, stirring occasionally. Beat egg; add rest of ingredients. Bring to a boil until thick, stirring constantly. Add vanilla and coconut; cool. Cut into squares and put filling in between. Roll in powdered sugar. Store in refrigerator.

Dorothy Troyer
STURGIS

ℑℭ☙ℑℭ☙ℑℭ

Kentucky Blue Grass
Fudge Brownie Pie

(This recipe is dedicated to the memory of Mrs. Robert W. Morse.)

Cream:
>½ cup oleo
>1 cup sugar
>2 eggs
>3 teaspoons vanilla

Mix:
>⅔ cup flour
>½ cup cocoa
>½ teaspoon baking powder
>½ teaspoon salt

Add the above ingredients to the creamed mixture. Stir in **1½ cups chopped nuts**.

In a greased 10-inch pie plate, bake the above for 30 minutes at 350°. Test. Do NOT overbake.

This is delicious!

>*Mrs. Robert W. Morse*
>STANWOOD

Chewy Cherry Brownies
(The idea to put the cherries over our favorite brownies came from a friend in Howell.)

⅓ cup butter
2 1-ounce squares unsweetened chocolate
1 cup sugar
2 eggs
⅓ teaspoon salt
½ cup flour, sifted
½ cup chopped nuts
1 teaspoon vanilla
½ cup chocolate chips (optional)
1 cup cherry pie filling

Melt butter and unsweetened chocolate in pan over low heat. Remove from heat and add remaining ingredients, except chocolate chips and cherry pie filling. Mix well.

Pour into an 8x8x2-inch pan. Sprinkle with chocolate chips. Bake 20-25 minutes at 350°.

When cool, spoon cherry pie filling over brownies and then enjoy!

Janet Pugno
LINCOLN PARK

Frosted Chocolate Almond Brownies

(All of my family and friends are very fond of these brownies. One friend, in particular, thinks there are no others as good as these.)

4 ounces unsweetened chocolate
1½ cups sifted all-purpose flour
1 teaspoon baking powder
1 teaspoon salt
1 cup soft shortening
2 cups granulated sugar
4 eggs, unbeaten
1 teaspoon almond extract
1 cup sliced almonds

1. Preheat oven to 350°. Lightly grease 9x13-inch pan. Melt chocolate in top of double boiler over hot (not boiling) water. Set aside to cool.

2. Sift flour with baking powder and salt.

3. In medium bowl, using wooden spoon, beat shortening with sugar until light. Beat in eggs, one at a time. Add the almond extract and chocolate.

4. Stir in flour mixture and sliced almonds. Turn into prepared pan and bake 25 to 30 minutes, or until surface is firm to touch. (I use a cake tester). Cool in pan. Frost.

Chocolate Frosting

2 ounces unsweetened chocolate
4 tablespoons butter or margarine
4 tablespoons light cream (or half and half)
2 cups sifted confectioners sugar
1 teaspoon vanilla

1. Melt chocolate over hot (not boiling) water. Set aside to cool.

2. In small bowl, combine butter, cream and sugar. Beat until smooth. (I use an electric mixer.)

3. Stir in cooled chocolate. Add vanilla and blend well. Frost brownies.

Harriet Hull
Novi

Brownie Scrumpsch

(This is my grandmother's secret "cheer you up" brownies. These were what we served when someone got sick, when you got a little homesick or when the dog got hit by a car. These will surely cheer anyone–anytime!)

> **12 double graham crackers**
> **1 can evaporated condensed milk (Eagle Brand)**
> **1 package chocolate chips (12 ounces)**
> **4 ounces walnuts (chopped)**
> **1 teaspoon vanilla**
> **3 teaspoons hot water**

Crush graham crackers (with a rolling pin). Add chocolate chips, chopped nuts and condensed milk. Scrape the excess milk out of the can by adding the 3 teaspoons of hot water and then pouring into the bowl. Add 1 teaspoon vanilla. Combine the ingredients by hand.

Bake in a greased 9-inch square pan at 350° for approximately 20-25 minutes, until top springs back when touched.

Remove from oven; cut into squares and remove from pan. Cool on rack.

Rebecca Singer
ANN ARBOR

❖❖❖❖ Butch's Best Brownies ❖❖❖❖

3 1-ounce squares unsweetened chocolate
½ cup butter
1 can Eagle Brand sweetened condensed milk
2 eggs
1 cup sifted all-purpose flour
½ teaspoon baking powder
¼ teaspoon salt
1 teaspoon pure vanilla extract
1 cup chopped walnuts

–In the top of a double boiler over hot water, blend chocolate and butter.
–Remove from heat; stir in condensed milk
–Beat in eggs, one at a time.
–Sift together flour, baking powder and salt. Gradually add this to chocolate mixture; stir in well after each addition.
–Stir in vanilla.
–Fold in chopped nuts.
–Spread mixture in a well-greased 13x9x2-inch pan.
–Bake in a moderate oven at 350° for 25-30 minutes.
–Cool. Cut into squares.
–Makes 24 2-inch square brownies.

Bernard J. Schoof Jr.
HARPER WOODS

Jessica's Mocha-Mint Caramel Downfall

1 2-layer package chocolate cake mix
1 tablespoon Irish Mocha-Mint
   coffee beverage mix
½ cup chopped walnuts
1 5⅓-ounce can (⅔ cup) evaporated milk
¼ cup butter or margarine, melted
½ cup semi-sweet chocolate chips
½ cup caramel topping

   Combine dry cake mix, coffee mix and walnuts. Mix in
evaporated milk and melted butter or margarine.
   Spread half the mixture in greased 13x9-inch pan. Bake at 350°
for 10 minutes.
   Remove from oven.
   Sprinkle chocolate chips over crust. Drizzle with caramel topping.
Drop remaining batter over top by teaspoons. Spread to cover as best
you can–you may have some bare spots. Using your hands to form
flat pieces to lay on top may be helpful.
   Return to oven to bake 20-25 more minutes.
   Cool. Cut into bars.
   Makes 36 brownies.

Chocolate Malt Bars

1 ounce square unsweetened chocolate
½ cup shortening
¾ cup sugar
½ teaspoon vanilla
2 eggs
1 cup sifted all-purpose flour
½ cup chocolate flavored malted milk powder
½ teaspoon baking soda
½ teaspoon salt
½ cup chopped walnuts

Melt chocolate; cool. Cream together next 3 ingredients till fluffy. Beat in eggs. Blend in melted chocolate. Sift dry ingredients together. Stir into creamed mixture. Fold in nuts. Spread in greased 8x8x2-inch baking pan. Bake in 350°-oven for 20-25 minutes; cool. Frost with Malt Frosting.

Malt Frosting:

Cream **2 tablespoons soft butter** or **margarine, ¼ cup chocolate-flavored malted milk powder** and **a dash of salt.** Slowly beat in **1 cup sifted confectioners sugar** and **enough light cream** to make of spreading consistency (about 1½ tablespoons).
Makes about 32 bars.

Lonna R. Kletter
TROY

85

Chewy Chocolate Pudding Brownies

(This recipe was given to me by a friend several years ago. What was interesting about it was the pudding. It was worth trying because my family and friends just loved it.)

Sift:
- 2 cups flour
- 2 cups sugar
- ½ teaspoon salt

Heat to boiling in saucepan:
- 2 sticks oleo
- 1 cup water
- 3 tablespoons cocoa

Pour over flour mixture.

Meanwhile in a small bowl, mix together well:
- 2 eggs (beaten)
- ½ cup buttermilk
- 1 tablespoon soda
- 1 tablespoon vanilla

Combine with above mixture and mix well.

Finally blend in:
1 small package chocolate pudding (regular)
1 cup chopped nuts

Pour into large greased cookie sheet. Bake in 350°-oven for 20 to 25 minutes. Do not overbake.

Cream Cheese Frosting

1 package (3 ounces) cream cheese
½ cup butter or oleo
2 teaspoons vanilla
1 pound powdered sugar

Beat cream cheese, butter or oleo and vanilla together. Gradually add sugar, beating until frosting is of spreading consistency. Add **1 tablespoon water** at a time if necessary.

Vicki DeVaux
EAST TAWAS

Chocolate Butter Cream Brownies

2 square (2 ounces) unsweetened chocolate
½ cup butter or margarine
2 eggs
1 cup sugar
1 teaspoon vanilla
½ cup flour
¼ teaspoon salt

Melt chocolate with butter over hot water. Beat eggs and sugar well. Add vanilla. Stir in chocolate mixture. Mix in flour and salt, blending well.

Spread in greased 11x7-inch baking pan. Bake at 350° for 20-25 minutes. Cool in pan. Spread with Vanilla Cream Frosting.

Vanilla Cream Frosting

1½ cups sugar
⅓ cup butter or margarine
½ cup half-and-half
1 teaspoon vanilla

Bring sugar, butter and half-and-half to a boil in heavy saucepan. Cook until a candy thermometer reaches 236° (the soft ball stage).

Set pan in ice water in the sink until mixture cools. Beat in vanilla; continue beating until creamy and smooth. Spread over brownies.

Spread a thin coating of Chocolate Glaze over icing.

Chocolate Glaze

3 squares unsweetened chocolate
3 tablespoons butter or margarine

Melt chocolate and butter over hot water. Spread over icing. Place brownies in refrigerator to set. When firm, cut into squares. Makes about 20 brownies.

Spice Gumdrop Bars

(I've been baking and cooking since the age of nine, and I love it. This recipe was just made up on the spur of the moment and everyone loved it.)

4 beaten eggs
2 cups brown sugar
1 tablespoon cold water
2 cups flour
Dash of salt
1 teaspoon nutmeg
1 cup chopped gumdrops
1 cup chopped nuts

Mix eggs and sugar. Add water. Mix flour with other dry ingredients. Sift over gumdrops and nuts, tossing so each piece is covered with flour. Add remaining flour and egg mixture. Mix.
Spread in a 2x8x13-inch pan. Bake in 300° oven for one hour.

Mrs. Marion F. Wells
LAKE ORION

Mint Stick Brownies

2 squares unsweetened chocolate
½ cup butter or margarine
2 eggs, well beaten
1 cup sugar
¼ teaspoon peppermint flavoring
½ cup flour
1/8 teaspoon salt
½ cup chopped nuts
Mint Frosting
Glaze Topping

Combine chocolate and butter; melt in double boiler over hot water. Cool. Add eggs, sugar, flavoring, flour, salt and nuts; blend well. Pour batter into a well-greased 9-inch square pan. Bake at 350° for 20-25 minutes; cool.

Spread with Mint Frosting; refrigerate. Spread Glaze Topping over frosting; refrigerate.

Yield: 16 (2-inch) squares.

Mint Frosting

2 tablespoons butter, softened
1 cup powdered sugar
Few drops green food coloring
1 tablespoon whipping cream or half and half
½ teaspoon peppermint flavoring

Combine all ingredients; blend until creamy. Spread on cooled brownies. Refrigerate while making glaze.

Glaze Topping;

1 square unsweetened chocolate
1 tablespoon butter

Combine ingredients and melt in double boiler; blend well. Spread over mint frosting.

Nancy Cornell
MILAN

90

Sequoia Brownies

(Everyone I have ever served these to has asked for the recipe. I have been making these for over 25 years.)

1 cup (2 sticks) butter
4 squares unsweetened chocolate
2 boxes (1 pound each) dark brown sugar
1⅓ cups sifted all-purpose flour
½ teaspoon salt
4 eggs
1 tablespoon vanilla
2 cups chopped walnuts

1. Prepare pan. Line a 15x10x1-inch jelly roll pan with wax paper.

2. Combine butter, chocolate and sugar in top of double boiler over hot water, stirring until chocolate is melted and sugar dissolved. Remove from heat, pour into medium sized bowl.

3. Stir in sifted flour and salt. Add eggs, one at a time, beating well after each. Stir in vanilla and walnuts. Spread evenly in pan.

4. Place pan in oven. Turn oven on 300°. Bake for 45 minutes. Turn oven off and let pan stand for another 15 minutes. Remove from oven. Loosen brownies around sides of pan; invert pan onto cookie sheet. Peel off wax paper. Let cool. Cut into 2x1-inch pieces. Store in tightly covered container, or wrap and freeze.

Lillian E. DeHate
BEAVERTON

Bourbon Brownies

¾ cup flour
¼ teaspoon salt
¼ teaspoon baking soda
⅓ cup butter
½ cup sugar
2 tablespoons milk
1 6-ounce package chocolate chips
1 teaspoon vanilla
2 eggs
1½ cups chopped nuts
4 tablespoons bourbon
Frosting

Preheat oven to 325°.

Combine flour, salt and baking soda in a bowl. Set aside.

Combine butter, sugar and milk in a saucepan. Heat just to boiling, stirring constantly. Remove from heat and add chocolate chips and vanilla. Mix until smooth.

Beat eggs, one at a time, into butter mixture. Add flour mixture gradually, mixing well. Stir in nuts.

Spread in a buttered 8 or 9-inch square pan. Bake for 25 to 30 minutes.

Cool and sprinkle with bourbon. Frost with frosting.

Makes about 25 brownies

(This recipe came into my possession when I lived back in Connecticut. The ingredients where intriguing and the results always brought raves from those who tasted the brownies. If one wishes to avoid the alcohol, they can flavor the brownie batter and frosting with liquor-flavored extracts or other flavors as desired.)

Frosting

½ cup soft butter
1 teaspoon rum extract
2 cups confectioners sugar
1 tablespoon butter
1 6-ounce package chocolate chips

Mix butter, rum extract and confectioners sugar together well. Spread over top of brownies. Refrigerate to set.

Put 1 tablespoon of butter and chocolate chips over hot water in a small saucepan. Stir and heat until melted.

Spread over the top of the chilled, frosted brownies.

Cynthia Goldman
SOUTHFIELD

Herman Brownies

(Remember Herman? How could you forget, huh? It's that stuff that ran all over your refrigerator and glued itself to the shelves. It's that stuff you made into 32 coffeecakes in 32 days. It's that stuff responsible for your first trip to Vic Tanny's.

Well, once more, heeeerrrrrreeeeeeee's Herman.)

    1 cup Herman
    2 cups sugar
    1 cup (1 stick) butter or margarine, softened
    2 eggs
    2 envelopes Nestles Choco-bake
    1 teaspoon vanilla
    1 cup flour
    ½ teaspoon cinnamon
    ¼ teaspoon salt
    ½ cup semi-sweet chocolate chips

Beat together until creamy Herman, sugar and butter. Blend in eggs, one at a time. Mix in chocolate and vanilla. Add flour, cinnamon and salt; beating until well blended.

Spread in greased 9x13-inch pan. Sprinkle with chocolate chips. Bake at 350° for 30-35 minutes.

Cool. Cut into squares.

(If you're feeling nostalgic, or just plain crazy, and want to get Herman going again, here's how.)

Combine **2 cups flour, 1 package dry yeast** and **2 cups warm water** in a glass or pottery bowl–do NOT use a metal one. Let stand in a warm place for 48 hours, stirring occasionally.

When it's yeasty smelling and bubbly, pour into a glass or pottery jar to store in the refrigerator.

Before using, let Herman stand in a warm place (a warm oven that has been turned off is ideal) until mixture is bubbly, about 3 hours. If starter separates, just stir before using.

Replace Herman with **1 cup flour** and **1 cup water** for every cup of mixture you remove.

Herman should be used at least once every 2 weeks to keep it going well.

Barbie-Bob's Brownies

(If you want to win a fellow's heart, this is what to feed him!!)

1 box brownie mix
1 8-ounce container of sour cream
1 6-ounce package chocolate chips

Prepare brownie mix according to instructions on package. Then add sour cream and chocolate chips. Mix thoroughly; pour into a 13x9-inch pan and bake according to package instructions. Bon appetit!!

(If I want them real fudgey, I add 12 ounces of chocolate chips instead of 6 ounces.)

Barbara Courier
LANSING

Fudge Marble Brownies

1 cup butter
4 squares unsweetened chocolate
2½ cups sugar
4 eggs
1 cup flour
½ teaspoon salt
1 cup walnuts
2 teaspoons vanilla
1 8-ounce package of cream cheese

Grease a 9x13-inch pan with butter. In a 2-quart heavy saucepan, melt butter and chocolate over low heat. Beat in 3 eggs and 2 cups sugar. Add flour, nuts, salt and 1 teaspoon vanilla. Mix with a wooden spoon and spread in pan.

In a small bowl, beat cream cheese and ½ cup sugar. Add 1 egg and 1 teaspoon vanilla. Beat until well mixed. With a large spoon drop mixture onto the batter. Swirl with a knife. Bake at 350° for 40-45 minutes.

Maureen Robinson
PLYMOUTH, MI

LEROY IS A REAL SQUARE!

Powdered Milk Brownies

(I have eight children, so I do quite a bit of baking. And of all the brownie recipes I have used, they all like this the best–it has the moistest and smoothest texture, and the flavor is just super.)

    1½ cups flour
    2½ cups sugar
    1 teaspoon baking powder
    ½ teaspoon salt
    ⅔ cup powdered milk
    1 cup oleo (softened)
    ½ cup cocoa
    4 eggs
    4 tablespoons water
    2 teaspoons vanilla
    1 cup chopped nuts (optional)

Combine all ingredients together and mix thoroughly with a wooden spoon. (Do not use mixer–it will ruin the texture.)

Pour into a lightly greased 9x13-inch pan. Bake in a preheated 350°-oven for 30-35 minutes.

Do not overbake. These are too delicious to ruin.

Gayle Stromer
CHASSELL

Grandma Bruno's Brownies

1 cup Crisco
4 squares chocolate
1½ cups sifted flour
1 teaspoon baking powder
1 teaspoon salt
4 eggs
2 cups sugar
2 teaspoons vanilla
¼ cup white corn syrup
1 cup chopped nuts (optional–I use them)

1. Melt Crisco and chocolate. Cool.
2. Sift dry ingredients together.
3. Beat eggs–add sugar–mix.
4. Add dry ingredients, vanilla and melted ingredients to above.
5. Mix well–add syrup–stir in nuts.
6. Pour into greased 9x13-inch pan. Bake 30-35 minutes at 350°. Cool and frost with favorite frosting.
(Do not overbake–brownies should be moist.)

Sue Pompian
Sterling Heights

98

Brownie Party Cake

(This is a handed down family recipe. It's my favorite because the recipe name speaks for itself–"party." Before I retired as an executive secretary in the administration office of our school system and it was my turn to treat, I was always asked to bring brownies. I was always happy to do so as the recipe would serve the entire group. Also, I think the frosting and sour cream adds a different and pleasing flavor over other brownies.)

        2 cups sugar
        2 cups flour
        ½ teaspoon salt
        2 sticks margarine
        1 cup water
        4 tablespoons cocoa
        2 eggs
        ½ cup sour cream
        1 teaspoon soda

In large bowl, place sugar, flour and salt. In saucepan, place margarine, water and cocoa; bring to a boil. Add to mixture in the mixing bowl–mix well. Add eggs, sour cream and soda; mix well. Pour into well-greased 18x11½-inch jelly roll pan. Bake 20 minutes in 400° preheated oven.

Frosting

        1 stick margarine
        4 tablespoons cocoa
        6 tablespoons milk
        1 box powdered sugar
        1 teaspoon vanilla
        1 cup nuts

Place first three ingredients in saucepan. Heat until margarine melts and comes to a boil; boil 1 minute. Remove from heat. Add powdered sugar, vanilla and nuts. Pour over cake as soon as it comes from the oven.
Delicious!!!

                        Alberta E. Day
                        SAGINAW

No Bake Confetti Brownies

1 cup chopped walnuts or pecans
2 cups colored miniature marshmallows
3 cups graham cracker crumbs (about 38 squares)
1 cup confectioners sugar
2 packages (6 ounces each) semi-sweet chocolate pieces
1 cup evaporated milk
½ teaspoon peppermint extract

In a large bowl, mix together nuts, marshmallows, crumbs and confectioners sugar. In a saucepan, melt chocolate and evaporated milk over low heat, stirring until thick and smooth.

Remove from heat; add peppermint extract. (Reserve ½ cup chocolate mixture for frosting.) Add remainder to crumb mixture. Stir until all crumbs are moistened.

Turn into a buttered 8-inch square pan. Press down into pan.

Spread the reserved chocolate mixture over top. Chill until ready to serve.

Cut into pieces approximately 1x2 inches. Garnish with walnuts. Makes 32 brownies.

Marilyn J. Amidon
TRAVERSE CITY

Baby Butchies Brownies III

3 egg whites
¾ cup sugar
¾ cup fine chocolate wafer crumbs
½ cup chopped walnuts
1 teaspoon pure vanilla, divided
½ pint whipping cream
Grated chocolate

–Beat egg whites until soft peaks form.
–Gradually add sugar, and continue to beat until stiff peaks form.
–Fold in crumbs, chopped walnuts and ½ teaspoon vanilla
–Spread evenly into a greased 8x8x2-inch glass pan.
–Bake in a preheated oven for 35 minutes at 325°.
–Cool.
–Whip cream with remaining vanilla.
–Spread over brownie mixture.
–Sprinkle with grated chocolate
–Cut into squares.
–*Kids love these!*

Barbara Schoof
HARPER WOODS

Boston Brownies

1 cup sugar
⅓ cup butter
2 eggs
1 cup flour
1 teaspoon baking powder
2 squares (2 ounces) melted chocolate
¼ cup water
1 teaspoon vanilla
1 cup walnuts
½ cup raisins

Beat sugar and butter together until fluffy. Add eggs, beating well after each addition. Sift flour and baking powder into mixture. Blend well. Mix in chocolate, water and vanilla. Stir in walnuts and raisins.

Drop by spoonfuls onto waxed paper laid in shallow pan. Bake at 350° for 10 minutes.

Chocolate Cherry Brownies

1 package fudge cake mix
2 1-ounce can cherry fruit filling
1 teaspoon almond extract
2 eggs, beaten

Preheat oven to 350°.

Using solid shortening or margarine, grease and flour 13x9-inch pan.

In large bowl, combine first 4 ingredients. By hand, stir until well mixed. Pour into prepared pan.

Bake 20-25 minutes, or until toothpick comes out clean. While brownies cool, prepare frosting.

Frosting:

1 cup sugar
5 tablespoons butter or margarine
⅓ cup milk
6-ounce package (1 cup) semi-sweeet chocolate pieces

In small saucepan, combine sugar, butter and milk. Boil, stirring occasionally, 1 minute. Remove from heat; stir in chocolate pieces until smooth. Pour over partially cooled brownies.

Makes about 3 dozen bars

Vicki Rautio
Ishpeming

❖❖❖❖❖❖❖❖❖❖❖❖Dolores' Brownies❖❖❖❖❖❖❖❖❖❖❖❖❖

(This brownie recipe is by far the most fantastic and yet has the simplest method. They are moist, chewy and the flavor is a brownie lover's heaven. Needless to say, my family and friends have been delighted since I discovered them.)

Cook slowly for just about 5 minutes:
> **¾ cup cocoa**
> **1 cup margarine**

Remove from heat and add:
> **2 cups sugar**
> **1½ cups flour**
> **2 teaspoons vanilla**
> **4 eggs**
> **½ teaspoon salt**
> **1 cup chopped nuts**

Mix all ingredients together. Pour into a greased 9x13-inch pan. Bake for 30 minutes at 350°. About 5 minutes after removing from oven, spread brownies with frosting.

Frosting

Bring to a rolling boil:
> **¼ cup margarine**
> **¼ cup milk**
> **1 cup sugar**

Remove from heat and add:
> **⅔ cup chocolate chips**

Mix until melted and smooth.

Dolores C. Caram
Royal Oak

❖❖❖❖❖❖❖❖❖❖❖❖❖❖❖❖❖

Fudge Brownies a la Kathleen

6 ounces semi-sweet chocolate squares or morsels
½ cup butter
2 cups sugar
4 eggs
½ teaspoon salt
1 teaspoon vanilla
1 cup flour
¼ teaspoon baking powder
1 package (3¾ ounces) chocolate Jello instant pudding
1 cup chopped walnuts

Preheat oven to 350°.

In top of double boiler, melt butter and chocolate until smooth. Set aside to cool. In a small bowl, combine flour, chocolate pudding mix, baking powder and salt. In mixer, beat eggs. Add sugar slowly; beat until well blended. Add vanilla and butter/chocolate to egg mixture. Gradually blend in flour. Add walnuts.

Grease a 9x13-inch pan. Pour in batter. Decorate with walnut halves or pieces. Bake for 35 minutes in metal pan. If using glass pan, decrease baking time to 30 minutes. Cool, then cut into squares.

Leslie R. Shaw
DETROIT

Special People Brownies

(I like the name for my brownies very much since I wrote the recipe for an especially special person, my husband, Ron, who is most fond of the chocolate-peanut butter combination.)

1 cup butter or margarine
½ cup cocoa
2 cups sugar
4 eggs
1 cup sifted all-purpose flour
1 teaspoon rum extract
½ teaspoon salt
2 cups peanut butter chips
1 cup chopped pecans

In large saucepan melt butter; remove from heat. Blend in cocoa and sugar. Add eggs, one at a time, and beat until well-blended after each addition. Blend in flour, rum extract and salt. Stir in peanut butter chips and pecans.

Spoon into a greased 13x9-inch baking pan. Bake at 350° for 30 minutes, or until toothpick inserted in center comes out clean.

Yield: 24 brownies.

Mary B. Peters
CANTON

Dutch Brownies

(This is my favorite brownie recipe because I can use corn oil margarine and dry cocoa powder, both with no cholesterol content. It also does not take special ingredients--these are on my shelves all the time.)

    1 cup sugar
    2 tablespoons Dutch process (Droste) cocoa (If American cocoa is used, increase to at least 3 tablespoons.)
    1 teaspoon vanilla
    3 eggs, or equivalent in Egg Beaters
    ¾ cup flour
    ½ cup melted margarine
    ½ cup chopped nuts

Beat eggs. Add sugar. Stir in cocoa, flour, vanilla, nuts and melted margarine.

Bake in 9x13-inch pan at 350° for 30 minutes. Put foil over pan as soon as it gets out of the oven.

Chocolate Glaze:

    1 tablespoon melted margarine
    1 tablespoon cocoa
    1 cup powdered sugar
    Enough warm milk to make a smooth glaze

Mix and spread on brownies. Cut into squares.
(These freeze and store well.)

                        Hazel Bos
                        HOLLAND

Rainbow Brownies

(I believe in easy-to-prepare recipes. At the same time, they have to have eye appeal and be pleasing to the palate–just like these brownies)

> 1 package of prepared brownie mix
> 1 tablespoon orange juice
> 1 tablespoon brandy
> 1 tablespoon peanut butter
> Ready-to-spread white frosting
> 1 teaspoon peanut butter
> 1 teaspoon brandy
> ½ cup chopped peanuts
> Maraschino cherries

Follow package directions. Instead of water, add juice, brandy and peanut butter to mix. Spread in buttered baking pan and follow baking directions.

Add brandy and peanut butter to frosting. Mix and spread on cooled cake. Top with chopped nuts and maraschino cherries. Cut into bars.

Before you know, they are gone.

Lea Aronson
SOUTHFIELD

White Chocolate
Butterscotch Brownies

(White chocolate, by the way, is a misnomer since it contains no liquid chocolate and therefore does not comply with government standards for chocolate. It actually is made of vegetable fats instead of cocoa butter, and contains added flavors and vegetable coloring.

However, if you happen to like the flavor of white chocolate, I've included this recipe. Its texture is more cakelike than other brownies.)

2 cups flour
1 teaspoon baking powder
¼ teaspoon baking soda
1 teaspoon salt
½ cup butter or margarine, softened
1 cup brown sugar, packed
2 eggs
2 tablespoons milk
1 teaspoon vanilla
1⅓ cups coarsely chopped white chocolate
½ cup chopped walnuts (optional)

Sift together first four ingredients. Set aside.

Cream butter and brown sugar until light and fluffy. Add eggs, beating well. Blend in vanilla. Gradually beat in dry ingredients.

Stir in chunks of white chocolate and walnuts.

Spread batter in greased 8-inch baking pan. Bake at 325° for 30-35 minutes, or until done.

Grate about ¼ **cup white chocolate** over the top of brownies while cooling. Spread or just leave as is.

Cool. Cut into squares.

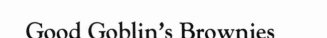

Good Goblin's Brownies

(This recipe was orginally created as a way to make use of a bountiful harvest of pie pumpkins in 1982. The family now requests it because of the moistness and rich flavor.)

Melt in saucepan over low heat:
  1 cup butter or margarine

Add:
  ½ cup cocoa
  1 cup pumpkin, canned

Bring to boil, stirring constantly. Remove from heat and set aside.

Mix together in large mixing bowl:
  2 cups flour
  2 cups sugar
  1 teaspoon baking soda
  ¼ teaspoon nutmeg

Stir into flour mixture:
  2 eggs
  ½ cup buttermilk or sour milk
  2 teaspoons vanilla

Add cocoa mixture. Stir until well blended. Pour into jelly roll pan (15½x10½x7/8 inches). Bake at 375° for 20 minutes.
While brownies are baking, prepare frosting.

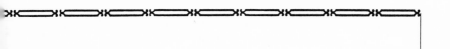

Frosting

Melt in saucepan over low heat:
   ¼ **cup butter**

Add:
   3 tablespoons cocoa
   ¼ **cup canned pumpkin**

Cook and stir until boiling. Remove from heat.

Beat into cocoa mixture:
   2½ **cups powdered sugar, sifted**
   ½ **teaspoon vanilla**

Pour frosting over HOT brownies. Spread evenly.
Cool. Cut in bars–1¾x2 inches.

Clara Lauinger
PONTIAC

Katherine Hepburn Brownies

2 squares unsweetened chocolate
¼ pound margarine
1 cup sugar
2 eggs
½ teaspoon vanilla
1 cup chopped nuts
¼ cup all-purpose flour
¼ teaspoon salt

Preheat oven to 325°.

Melt chocolate and margarine over very low heat in a saucepan. Remove from heat and stir in sugar. Beat in eggs and vanilla. Quickly stir in nuts, flour and salt.

Spread batter in well-greased 8x8-inch square baking pan and bake for 40-45 minutes. Remove and place on rack to cool. Cut into squares.

Michelle DeLand-Duffy
WARREN

YOU FUDGED THESE
ANSWERS DIDN'T YOU!

TEST

Sinful Brownies

(I always contribute a batch of these when our choir members have a candy sale, as I am not a candy maker. However, they sell very well–even along-side fudge. These are real diet-busters!)

Melt, then cool:
> **1 cup (6 ounces) chocolate chips**
> **½ cup margarine (1 stick)**
> **1 teaspoon vanilla**

Mix together:
> **⅔ cup brown sugar**
> **2 eggs**

Sift, then mix with above ingredients:
> **1½ cups flour**
> **2 teaspoons baking powder**

Add:
> **2 cups mini-marshmallows**
> **1 cup (6 ounces) chocolate chips.**
> **1 cup nuts, broken**

Spread in cake sheet pan 13x9 inches. Bake at 350° about 20-25 minutes.

DON'T overbake; center will be jiggly but will set when cool. *Enjoy!*

Harriet Betwee
ROMULUS

❖❖❖❖❖❖❖❖❖❖ Mint Swirl Brownies ❖❖❖❖❖❖❖❖❖❖

1 3-ounce package cream cheese, softened
¼ cup butter or margarine, softened
¾ cup sugar
2 eggs
⅔ cup flour
½ teaspoon baking powder
¼ teaspoon salt
⅓ cup chopped nuts
1 ounce unsweetened chocolate, melted and cooled
½ teaspoon peppermint extract
Several drops green food coloring
Chocolate Glaze

Cream together cream cheese, butter and sugar; beat in eggs. Stir together flour, baking powder and salt; stir into creamed mixture.

Spoon ½ of batter into another bowl; stir in nuts and chocolate. Drop chocolate batter from tablespoon checkerboard fashion into greased 9x9x2-inch baking pan.

To remaining batter, stir in extract and food coloring. Spoon green batter into open spaces in baking pan. Swirl with spatula to marble; do not overmix.

Bake at 350° for 15-20 minutes. Cool. Pour chocolate glaze over top.

Chocolate Glaze

Melt **1-ounce square unsweetened chocolate** and **1 tablespoon butter or margarine** over low heat; stir constantly.

Remove from heat; stir in **1 cup powdered sugar** and ½ **teaspoon vanilla** till crumbly. Blend in enough **boiling water (about 2 tablespoons)** till of pouring consistency.

Debbie Gronow
TROY

114

Chocolate Chip Fudge Brownies
with Mocha Frosting

½ cup butter or margarine
1 cup granulated sugar
1 teaspoon vanilla
2 eggs
2 1-ounce squares unsweetened chocolate
¾ cup all-purpose flour
1 cup chocolate chips

In medium saucepan, melt butter and chocolate over very low heat. Remove from heat; stir in sugar.

Blend in eggs one at a time. Add vanilla. Stir in flour; mix well. Stir in chocolate chips.

Spread in greased 8x8x2-inch pan. Bake at 350° for 25-30 minutes. Be careful not to overbake. Cool.

Frost with Mocha Frosting.

Mocha Frosting:

Cream ¼ cup butter or margarine, 2 tablespoons cocoa, 2 teaspoons instant coffee powder, dash of salt. Beat in 2½ cups sifted confectioners sugar, 1½ teaspoons vanilla and enough milk for spreading consistency.

Frost brownies with ½ of frosting. Store rest in refrigerator for next batch of brownies.

Enid Comito
CANTON

Yummy Brownies

(Several decades ago, when I drove Girl Scouts to their meetings, one mother served the best brownies I ever tasted, and she gave me the recipe. Any brownie is my favorite cookie, but yummies are special.)

In a 9x12-inch pan, melt:
   –1 stick of oleomargarine

Spread:
   –1 cup graham cracker crumbs over this

Spread:
   –1 cup coconut

Spread:
   –1 package (6 ounces) chocolate chips evenly

Spread:
   –1 cup walnuts

Pour:
   –1 can Eagle Brand condensed milk over entire pan

Bake 30 minutes at 350°. Cool completely, then cut into squares.

Eve Dishell
Oak Park

🐝 Princess Brownies 🐝

1 package family size brownie mix
1 8-ounce package Philadelphia brand cream cheese,
   softened
⅓ cup sugar
½ teaspoon vanilla
1 egg

Prepare brownie mix as directed on package.

Combine softened cream cheese and sugar; mix till well blended. Stir in vanilla and eggs. Spread half of brownie batter on bottom of greased 9x13-inch pan. Cover with creamed cheese mixture. Spoon on remaining brownie batter.

Bake at 350° for 35-40 minutes. Cool.

Makes 2 dozen, 1½-inch squares.

Judy Ballen
WEST BLOOMFIELD

Theresa's Favorite Brownies
(Creme de Menthe)

¾ butter
4 squares unsweetened chocolate
1 tablespoon Creme de Menthe
3 eggs
1 cup white sugar
¾ cup brown sugar
1 teaspoon vanilla
1¼ cup flour
1 teaspoon baking powder
1 cup chopped walnuts

Melt butter, chocolate and Creme de Menthe together.
Beat eggs well. Add sugar, brown sugar and vanilla. Mix well.
Add chocolate mixture. Stir in flour, baking powder and walnuts.
Mix together and pour in greased and floured 9x13-inch pan. Bake at
350° for 20-25 minutes.

Dolores Buchholz
HOWELL

❋❋❋ Heavenly Brownies ❋❋❋

1¼ cups sifted flour
½ teaspoon baking powder
½ teaspoon salt
½ cup lard
3 squares chocolate
2 eggs
1 cup sugar
1 cup chopped walnuts
1 cup marshmallow tidbits
1 teaspoon vanilla

Grease bottom of 8x12-inch baking pan. Sift flour, baking powder and salt. Melt lard and chocolate. Beat eggs and add sugar gradually. Add lard-chocolate mixture and vanilla. Beat well. Add sifted dry ingredients and nuts.

Pour into greased pan. Bake in slow (325°) oven for 25-30 minutes.

While brownies are still warm, top with marshmallows to partially melt them. Pour hot chocolate glaze (below) over marshmallows. Spread evenly until frosting and marshmallows completely cover brownies.

Chocolate Glaze

2 tablespoons butter
2 squares chocolate
2 cups sifted 10xxx sugar
1/8 teaspoon salt
½ teaspoon vanilla
3 tablespoons coffee

Melt butter and chocolate. Add confectioners sugar, salt, vanilla and coffee. Beat vigorously about 3 minutes or until glossiness disappears.

June Ahlin
ESCANABA

Jamaican Brownies

1 package (22 ounces) fudge brownie mix
1 can (15¼ ounces) pineapple tidbits, drained
¼ cup firmly packed brown sugar
¼ cup flour
2 tablespoons margarine or butter
⅓ cup chopped walnuts

Prepare brownie mix as package directs; fold in pineapple. Spread in greased 13x9-inch pan. Combine sugar and flour; cut in margarine or butter. Add nuts and sprinkle over batter. Bake at 350° for 40 minutes. Cool. Cut into squares. Makes 12 brownies.

Mary Binder Antoncew
DETROIT

Marshmallow Brownies

Preheat oven to 350°. Using solid shortening, grease bottom and sides of 9-inch square baking pan.

Melt in 3-quart saucepan over medium heat, stirring constantly:
½ cup (half 6-ounce package) butterscotch pieces
¼ cup butter or margarine

Remove from heat; cool to lukewarm.

Lightly spoon into measuring cup:
¾ cup flour

Add to butterscotch mixture in saucepan:
⅓ cup firmly packed brown sugar
1 teaspoon baking powder
¼ teaspoon salt
½ teaspoon vanilla
1 egg

Mix well.

Fold into butterscotch batter just until combined, about 5 strokes:

1 cup miniature marshmallows
1 cup (6-ounce package) semi-sweet chocolate pieces
¼ cup chopped nuts

Spread in greased pan.
Bake for 20-25 minutes. Do NOT over bake. Center will be jiggly but become firm upon cooling.

A.B.C.
Detroit

Rocky Road Fudge Brownies

(I first tasted these in college–my roommate's mother sent her a batch.
asked for the recipe, then made some modifications. This recipe is always
high on the top of my baking request list.)

Base:

½ cup margarine or butter
1 ounce (1 square) unsweetened chocolate,
   or pre-melted envelope
1 cup flour
1 cup sugar
1 teaspoon baking powder
1 teaspoon vanilla
2 eggs

Filling:

8-ounce package cream cheese, softened,
   reserve 2 ounces for frosting
¼ cup margarine or butter, softened
½ cup sugar
2 tablespoons all-purpose flour
½ teaspoon vanilla
1 egg
¾ cup chopped nuts
6-ounce package (1 cup) semi-sweet chocolate chips

Frosting:

2 cups miniature marshmallows
¼ cup margarine or butter
¼ cup milk
1 ounce (1 square) unsweetened chocolate,
   or pre-melted envelope
Reserved 2 ounces cream cheese
3 cups powdered milk
1 teaspoon vanilla

Heat oven to 350°.

Grease and flour 13x9-inch pan.

In large saucepan, melt margarine and chocolate over low heat. ghtly spoon flour into measuring cup; level off. Add remaining base gredients; mix well. Spread in prepared pan.

In small bowl, combine all filling ingredients, except nuts and ocolate chips. Beat 1 minute at medium speed until smooth and ffy. Stir in nuts.

Spread over chocolate mixture; sprinkle evenly with chocolate ips. Bake at 350° for 25-35 minutes, or until toothpick inserted in nter, comes out clean.

Sprinkle marshmallows over top. Return to oven; bake 2 minutes nger.

In large saucepan, melt ¼ cup margarine, 1 ounce chocolate, milk d reserved cream cheese over low heat.

Remove from heat. Stir in remaining frosting ingredients until ooth. Immediately pour frosting over marshmallows and swirl with ife to marble. Chill until firm

Cut into bars.

Makes 36 bars. One bar = 210 calories.

Vanessa Starke
CANTON

Zucchini Fudge Brownies

3 eggs
2 cups sugar
1 cup oil
2 teaspoons vanilla
2 cups grated, peeled zucchini
2 cups flour
2 teaspoons baking soda
2 teaspoons cinnamon
4 tablespoons cocoa
¼ teaspoon salt
1 cup chopped nuts

Preheat oven to 350°.

Beat eggs, sugar, oil, vanilla and zucchini. Sift dry ingredients; add to creamed mixture. Bake in a greased, floured sheet cake pan 20 minutes.

Frost while warm.

Frosting:

1 stick margarine
4 tablespoons cocoa
6 tablespoons milk
1 package confectioners sugar

Combine first three ingredients in a small saucepan and cook on low boil for 2 minutes. With a mixer, add confectioners sugar. Beat until creamy. Spread on warm brownies.

Cut and enjoy.

Klaren Gerhart
BLOOMFIELD HILLS

Hershey Syrup Brownies

(These do go quickly. They are favorites of my son and all his friends.)

1 stick margarine
1 cup sugar
4 eggs
1 teaspoon vanilla
1 can Hershey chocolate syrup (regular size)
1 cup flour
½ cup chopped nuts

Mix the margarine and sugar well. Add eggs and vanilla; mix well. Add flour, syrup and nuts, mixing after each addition. Pour into 9x13-inch cake pan and bake at 350° for 40-50 minutes.

Easy Fudge Frosting

6 tablespoons margarine
6 tablespoons milk
1½ cup sugar

Bring to a rolling boil, beating vigorously–beat and boil for just 30 seconds. Add **½ cup chocolate chips** and beat until it reaches spreading consistency. (Half of this frosting recipe is adequate if you prefer.)

Monna Ayers
ALBION

Bess Truman's Brownies

(One woman, attending a White House tea, took some of these brownies home. She tried 10 different versions before finding this one that came the closest. I have made different brownie recipes in the last 20 years, but we still like Bess Truman's the best. This recipe is from a woman's magazine.)

Preheat oven to 350°.

> ½ cup butter or margarine
> 1 cup sugar
> 2 eggs
> 1 teaspoon vanilla
> 2 envelopes unsweetened chocolate
> ¾ cup cake flour
> ½ teaspoon salt
> ½ teaspoon baking powder
> 1 cup coarsely chopped nuts

Cream butter or margarine with sugar until light and fluffy. Add eggs and the vanilla. Beat until smooth. Blend in chocolate.

Sift together cake flour, baking powder and salt. Stir into creamed mixture with coarsely chopped nuts.

Bake in well-greased 8-inch square pan for 30 minutes or until cake springs back when touched lightly in center. Cool in pan, then cut into 16 2-inch squares.

Delicious plain or with whipped cream on top. These are plump with nuts, very delicate.

Mrs. Margaret Peters
New Boston

Brownie Torte

(I received this recipe from my friend, Betty. It makes a nice dessert for a large dinner party or just for the family.)

Beat **3 egg whites, ½ teaspoon vanilla and dash salt** to soft peaks. Gradually add **¾ cup sugar**; beat to stiff peaks. Fold in **¾ cup fine chocolate wafer crumbs** and **½ cup chopped walnuts**.

Spread in buttered 9-inch pie plate. Bake in a slow oven (325°) for 5 minutes.

Cool well; top with **sweetened whipped cream**. Chill 3 to 4 hours. Trim with chocolate curls.

Mary A. Rogers
FARMINGTON HILLS

Chocolate Cinnamon Brownies

2 cups flour, sifted
1 teaspoon baking powder
Dash salt
1⅓ cups sugar, divided
4 teaspoons ground cinnamon, divided
1 teaspoon vanilla
1 cup butter or margarine, softened
1 egg
1 egg, separated
1 6-ounce package (1 cup) semi-sweet chocolate chips
½ cup chopped nuts

In a large bowl, mix together flour, baking powder, salt, 1 cup sugar and 3 teaspoons cinnamon. Blend in vanilla, butter, egg and 1 egg yolk, mixing well.

Spread evenly in a lightly greased 15x10-inch jelly roll pan. Lightly beat egg white; brush over mixture.

Mix together remaining ⅓ cup sugar, 1 teaspoon cinnamon, chocolate chips and nuts. Sprinkle over top.

Bake at 350° for 25-30 minutes. Cool. Cut into bars.

Makes about 75 1x2-inch bars.

✳ ⚜ ✳

Candy Bar Brownies

(This is a family recipe passed on to Lottie by her mother. Every two or three months she sends her grandson, stationed with the Navy in Hawaii, a package of them. The Navy men call them "Deeeleeeecious.")

Sift together **1 cup, plus 2 tablespoons flour** and **1/8 teaspoon salt.**

Melt **2 double chocolate covered coconut candy bars** (**Mound's Coconut Bars**) with **½ cup Crisco** over hot water, stirring occasionally to blend. Blend in **1 cup sugar** and **1 teaspoon vanilla.** Add **2 unbeaten eggs,** one at a time. Beat well.

Blend in the dry ingredients. Mix thoroughly. Stir in **½ cup nuts.**

Turn into well-greased 9x9x2-inch pan. Bake in oven (350°) 25-30 minutes. Cut into bars or squares.

Lottie Sikora
HAMTRAMCK

Applesauce Brownies I

2 1-ounce squares unsweetened chocolate
½ cup shortening or oleo
1 cup sugar
2 eggs, well beaten
⅔ cup applesauce
1 teaspoon vanilla
1 cup flour (sifted)
½ teaspoon baking powder
¼ teaspoon salt
¼ teaspoon baking soda
½ cup chopped pecans or walnuts

Melt together chocolate and shortening. Blend in sugar, eggs applesauce and vanilla. Sift dry ingredients. Stir into chocolate mixture. Add nuts. Put into greased 9x13-inch pan. Bake 35-40 minutes at 350°.

Frosting

Put in a pan on stove. Bring to a boil:
   1 stick oleo
   1 tablespoon cocoa
   6 tablespoons milk
Add:
   1-pound box 10xxx sugar
   1 teaspoon vanilla
   ½ cup chopped nuts

Put on brownies while still hot.

Sylvia Green
TROY

Applesauce Brownies II

2 squares (1 ounce each) unsweetened chocolate
½ cup butter or margarine
1 cup packed brown sugar
½ cup applesauce
2 eggs
1 teaspoon vanilla
1⅓ cups Bisquick baking mix
¼ teaspoon baking soda
½ cup chopped nuts

Heat chocolate and butter or margarine in a 2-quart saucepan over low heat, stirring constantly, until melted. Remove from heat and cool.

Mix in brown sugar, applesauce, eggs and vanilla. Stir in baking mix and baking soda.

Spread in rectangular pan 13x9x2 inches which has been greased. Sprinkle with nuts.

Bake at 350° for about 25-30 minutes–until brownies begin to pull away from sides of pan.

Cool.

Cut into 1½-inch squares.

Makes about 4 dozen.

Geraldine Tardiff
COLDWATER

Applesauce Brownies III

(This is actually more of a cake than a fudge-type brownie. But these little nummies are unbelievably moist–and they stay that way. No frosting needed on these yummers.)

> 1¼ cups sugar
> ½ cup butter
> 2 cups flour
> ½ teaspoon cinnamon
> 1¼ teaspoons baking soda
> 2 ounces melted unsweetened chocolate
> 2 cups applesauce
> 2 eggs
> ½ cup chopped walnuts
> 6-ounce package chocolate chips

Beat sugar and butter together. Sift dry ingredients. Add to sugar and butter with chocolate, applesauce and eggs. Beat well. Pour into greased 9x13-inch pan. Sprinkle with walnuts and chocolate chips. Bake at 350° for 30 minutes.

Cut into squares and eat up.

Chocolate Syrup Brownies with Chocolate Kahlua Glaze

1 cup sugar
½ cup butter or margarine, softened
4 eggs
1 16-ounce can chocolate flavored syrup
1¼ cups all-purpose flour
1 cup chopped walnuts

In mixing bowl, cream together sugar and softened butter till light and fluffy. Add eggs; beat well. Stir in chocolate-flavored syrup and flour till blended. (Batter will look curdled.) Stir in chopped nuts.

Pour mixture into greased 13x9x2-inch baking pan. Bake at 350° 30-35 minutes. Cool slightly; top with chocolate glaze. Cool; cut into bars.

Makes 32 brownies.

Chocolate Kahlua Glaze

⅔ cup sugar
3 tablespoons Kahlua
3 tablespoons butter or margarine
½ cup semi-sweet chocolate pieces

Combine sugar, Kahlua and butter. Bring to boiling; boil for 30 seconds. Remove from heat; stir in semi-sweet chocolate pieces till melted (mixture will be thin). Immediately pour atop brownies.

Janise Mapes
WALLED LAKE

❖❖❖❖❖❖❖❖❖❖❖ Beverly's Brownies ❖❖❖❖❖❖❖❖❖❖❖

(A friend of mine in Phoenix gave me this recipe. She had gotten it from a friend Houston. We like it because the brownies are so rich.)

> 2 cups sugar
> 5 eggs
> ½ cup cocoa
> 1 ¼ cups oil
> 1 ½ cups flour
> 1 teaspoon salt
> 2 cups chopped nuts
> 1 teaspoon vanilla
> Miniature marshmallows

Mix the sugar and eggs. Add the cocoa and oil; beat well. Add flour, salt, nuts and vanilla; mix well. Place in greased 12x13-inch pan (9x13-inch can also be used). Bake in 350°-oven for 20 minutes or until done.

Cover with miniature marshmallows; bake for 2 minutes longer. Cool.

Frosting:

> 1 cup (packed) brown sugar
> 2 tablespoons cocoa
> ½ cup water ·
> ½ cup margarine
> Powdered sugar (about a box)

Mix the brown sugar, cocoa and water in a small saucepan; boil for 2 minutes. Add the margarine and enough powdered sugar to thicken; spread on brownie mixture.

Cool; cut into squares.

Karen Hedgecorth
SOUTHFIELD

134

Caramel Filled Brownies

1 box German chocolate cake mix
6 ounces chocolate chips
⅔ cup evaporated milk
½ cup broken walnuts
1 bag caramels
¾ cup butter, melted

Mix *dry* cake mix with melted butter and ⅓ cup of the evaporated milk. Stir. Press into a greased and floured 13x9-inch pan. (Leave half of the mixture for later use.) Bake at 350° for 5 minutes.

Meanwhile, melt caramels with rest of evaporated milk.

Place a layer of chocolate chips, then nuts on brownie base. Pour caramel mixture over top. Top with rest of cake mix.

It's easiest to pat out sections in your hands and randomly lay on top of caramel.

Bake at 350° for 20 minutes more.

JoAnn Hoag
JACKSON

Peanut Butter Brownies I

(My family likes the peanut butter flavor in these.)

   2 eggs
   1 cup granulated sugar
   ½ cup brown sugar
   ¼ cup peanut butter
   2 tablespoons margarine
   1 teaspoon vanilla
   1⅓ cups unsifted flour
   1 teaspoon baking powder
   ½ teaspoon salt
   2 tablespoons chopped peanuts

Combine eggs, sugars, peanut butter, margarine and vanilla. Beat at medium speed until thoroughly blended. Add flour, baking powder and salt. Continue mixing until mixture is smooth.

Spread batter in a greased pan (9-inch square) and sprinkle with chopped nuts.

Bake in oven at 350° for 30 minutes.

Cut into squares while warm.

Amanda E. Kranich
DEARBORN

Peanut Butter Brownies II

1 cup peanut butter
½ cup (1 stick) butter or margarine, softened
2 cups brown sugar
3 eggs
1 teaspoon vanilla
1 cup flour, sifted
¼ teaspoon salt

Beat peanut butter, butter and sugar in a bowl until creamy. Mix in eggs and vanilla. Add in flour and salt, mixing well.

Spread in greased 9x13-inch pan. Bake at 350° for 30-35 minutes, or until golden brown.

Makes 24 brownies.

Peanut Butter Brownies III

1 cup sifted all purpose flour
½ teaspoon salt
½ cup (1 stick) butter or margarine, softened
1 cup sugar
4 eggs
1 teaspoon vanilla
1 can (16 ounces) chocolate syrup
¼ cup smooth or crunchy peanut butter
1 tablespoon butter or margarine, melted
2 squares (2 ounces) semisweet chocolate
½ tablespoon butter or margarine

1. Preheat oven to moderate (350°) setting. Grease a 13x9x2-inch baking pan.
2. Sift flour and salt onto wax paper.
3. Beat butter, sugar and eggs in a large bowl until light and fluffy; stir in vanilla.
4. Stir in flour and salt just until no streaks of white remain. Stir in chocolate syrup. Pour into prepared pan.
5. Bake in preheated moderate oven (350°) for 25 minutes, or until center springs back when lightly touched with fingertip. Cool completely in a pan on wire rack.
6. Mix peanut butter with 1 tablespoon melted butter; spread mixture evenly over top of brownies.
7. Melt chocolate with remaining butter in a small bowl over hot, not boiling water. Drizzle chocolate across peanut butter in lines 1-inch apart. Draw wooden pick or thin spatula across lines. Let chocolate set before cutting into 24 bars.

Orchard Alternative School
MONROE

Quick & Easy Marshmallow Brownies

2 sticks oleo
½ cup cocoa
4 eggs
2 teaspoons vanilla
½ teaspoon salt
1½ cups flour
2 cups sugar
¾ of a 13-ounce jar of marshmallow creme

In small saucepan, melt the oleo and cocoa together. In larger bowl, blend eggs, sugar and vanilla together. Add flour, salt and the cocoa-oleo mixture. Mix about 2 minutes (just until blended).

Grease a 9x13-inch pan. Spread evenly in pan. Mixture will be thick. (The tip of a fork works great in spreading.) Bake for 20-25 minutes at 350°. (Test with toothpick.)

While hot, spoon, at random, the marshmallow creme. Let sit, before spreading, about 2 minutes until marshmallow begins to melt. Then gently spread over the brownies. Let cool completely before topping with the frosting.

(The marshmallow creme won't look pretty like a topping, as it is NOT the topping. Sometimes I add more than the ¾ jar if needed to cover, sometimes less.)

Frosting

¼ cup cocoa
¾ stick melted oleo
2½ cups powdered sugar
1 tablespoon milk

Mix until creamy. Spread gently on top of marshmallow brownies.

Cut and serve after an hour or more.

Faye Carriger
PONTIAC

Chocolate Waffle Brownies

(Great with ice cream in the middle for an ice cream sandwich.)

1¼ cups sifted cake flour
½ teaspoon salt
6 tablespoons cocoa
1 tablespoon baking powder
2 eggs
¾ cup half and half
¼ cup melted butter
½ teaspoon vanilla extract
½ cup sugar
2 stiff-beaten egg whites

Sift flour, salt, cocoa and baking powder together.
Beat whole eggs with half and half.
Mix in butter, vanilla and sugar.
Blend into flour mixture.
Gently fold in egg whites.
Bake in preheated waffle iron.
Makes 3 10-inch waffles.

❧ Double Chocolate Pecan Brownies ❧

(This recipe was given to me by a very dear friend years ago who is now deceased. My family and friends, and especially children, love these brownies. I am always asked to bake them for school and community functions. They are delicious!)

Sift together and set aside:
>1 ¼ cups flour
>½ teaspoon soda
>½ teaspoon salt

Cream:
>½ cup butter or margarine (1 stick)
>½ cup brown sugar, well-packed
>¼ cup granulated sugar

Add:
>1 egg
>½ teaspoon vanilla

Mix well. Blend in dry ingredients. Spread in ungreased 9x13-inch pan. Bake at 350° for about 15 minutes.

Remove from oven and immediately sprinkle with **6 ounces semi-sweet chocolate bits**. Let stand 2 minutes, then spread to cover.

Frosting:

Combine in top of double boiler:
>**6 ounces semi-sweet chocolate bits**
>**⅓ cup maple syrup**
>**⅓ cup butter**
>**1 teaspoon vanilla**
>**¼ teaspoon salt**

Stir until melted and smooth. Add **1 cup chopped pecans (or walnuts)** and stir. Spread evenly over pan.

Bake at 350° for 8 minutes.

Cool. Cut into 1-inch squares or desired size.

Wanda Utsler
READING

Chocolate Microwave Brownies I

(I've been making these for years. Nothing fancy–just your basic chocolate brownie; superquick for a fast-advancing brownie attack.)

> 2 ounces unsweetened chocolate
> 1/3 cup shortening
> 1 cup sugar
> 2 eggs
> 1/2 teaspoon vanilla
> 1/4 teaspoon baking powder
> 1 cup sifted flour
> 1/4 teaspoon salt
> 1/2 cup nuts

Melt chocolate in its paper in oven 1 1/2-2 minutes; let cool. Cream shortening and sugar. Add eggs, one at a time, beating well after each one. Add vanilla and chocolate; mix well.

Sift dry ingredients together and mix into chocolate mixture. Stir in nuts.

Spread dough in greased 8-inch round or square glass baking dish. Cover with a paper towel and bake 5 minutes, turning dish half way through the baking period.

Cool before cutting.

Makes about 16 brownies.

(For a variation, try some chocolate chips stirred into the batter in place of the nuts.)

Chocolate Microwave Brownies II

(Same song, different verse)

²⁄₃ cup butter of margarine
¾ cup flour
½ cup unsweetened cocoa
½ teaspoon baking powder
½ teaspoon salt
½ teaspoon cinnamon
1 cup sugar
2 eggs
1 tablespoon corn syrup
1 teaspoon vanilla
½ cup walnuts (optional)

In a medium bowl, microwave butter until softened–about 15 seconds.

Sift flour, cocoa, baking powder, salt and cinnamon together. Set aside.

Beat sugar, eggs, corn syrup and vanilla with butter. Add dry ingredients, beating until just blended. Stir in walnuts.

Spread in an 8x8-inch baking dish. Microwave 5-6 minutes, rotating dish once during baking time.

Blast Me To the Moon Chocolate Chip-Coconut Microwave Bars

(It's fairly easy to O.D. on these.)

½ cup butter or margarine, softened
½ cup brown sugar
¼ cup granulated sugar
2 eggs
2 teaspoons vanilla
1 teaspoon water
1¼ cups flour
½ teaspoon baking powder
Dash salt
1 cup (6-ounce package) semi-sweet chocolate chips
½ cup coconut
¼ cup chopped nuts

Cream together butter and sugars until light and fluffy. Beat in eggs and vanilla, mixing well. Sift together dry ingredients. Add to creamed mixture. Stir in ½ cup chocolate chips, and all the coconut and chopped nuts.

Spread in greased 8-inch glass baking dish. Sprinkle with remaining ½ cup chocolate chips.

Bake 6-7 minutes, turning dish once half way through baking time.

Cool. Cut into 20 bars.

Microwave Brownies From a Mix

Mix up brownies according to package directions. If using an 8-ounce mix, pour into a greased glass loaf pan and bake, turning once during cooking time, 3½-5 minutes. If using a 16-ounce size, pour into a greased 8-inch square or round glass baking dish. Bake, turning once during cooking time, for 6-8 minutes.

You have to really watch the brownies close when the end of the baking time nears; just 20 seconds too long and–BLAH–cardboard. Remember, these critters keep on baking after you take them out of the oven, so it's better to remove them when they look slightly underdone then to wait until they're crispy.

You'll notice that in my microwave directions I give only one heat instruction–bake. There's no high, medium or whatever. That's because my microwaves–I'm already on my second model after blowing out my first one from over-use–have had only one heating power...blast. However, it's worked fine for me for the past eight years. I'll just continue blasting brownies into the next century.

I like to doctor my mixes up with chocolate chips, nuts, coconut or most anything else I have on hand. Sometimes I frost them with a powdered sugar frosting; sometimes I eat them as is. It all depends on my mood.

So experiment. It's hard to go wrong as long as you remember not to bake the daylights out of these things.

Chocolate Butter Pecan Brownies

1 cup brown sugar, packed
½ cup granulated sugar
⅓ cup light corn syrup
½ cup butter
3 eggs
2 1-ounce squares unsweetened chocolate,
  melted and cooled
1 cup flour
¼ teaspoon salt
⅓ cup chopped pecans
16 pecan halves

Beat together sugars, corn syrup and butter until smooth. Add eggs, beating well after each addition. Blend in chocolate. Add flour and salt; mixing well.

Stir in chopped pecans. Pour into a greased 9-inch square baking pan. Place 16 pecan halves on top of batter in rows.

Bake at 350° 35-40 minutes, or until done. Cool in pan. Cut into 16 brownies.

Quick 'n Easy Brownies

4 ounces semisweet chocolate
2 sticks margarine
1½ cups broken pecan nutmeats
1¾ cups sugar
1 cup unsifted flour
4 large eggs
1 teaspoon vanilla

Melt chocolate and margarine in heavy pan; add pecans and stir until nuts are well coated.

Combine sugar, flour, eggs and vanilla. Mix only until well-blended. Do NOT beat.

Add chocolate-nut mixture and again mix carefully, not beating.

Turn into paper baking cups and bake at 325° for 35 minutes. Do not overbake.

No frosting needed.

Thelma Wagner
CHARLEVOIX

Texas-Size Brownies

(Theses are goodies that you never have any left over to take back home again!!!)

Bring to a boil:

> **2 sticks oleo**
> **1 cup water**
> **6 tablespoons cocoa**

Add:

> **2 cups sugar**
> **2 cups flour**
> **½ teaspoon salt**

Cool slightly.

Add:

> **2 eggs**
> **8 ounces sour cream**
> **1 teaspoon baking soda**
> **1 cup chopped nuts**

Beat well. Pour into 11x18-inch sheet cake pan. Bake 20 minutes at 350°.

Topping

Bring to boil:

> **1 stick oleo**
> **6 tablespoons cocoa**
> **6 tablespoons milk**

After you bring to boil, remove from heat and add:

> **1 pound confectioners sugar**
> **1 teaspoon vanilla**

Beat well. Spread on hot cake top with **chopped walnuts**. Cool. Cut into large squares.

Sharleen A. Kashouty
MADISON HEIGHTS

Butterscotch Brownies
with Meringue Topping

(These brownies have a meringue-like top. They are really delicious.)

Cream together:
>½ cup shortening
>1 cup sugar

Add:
>2 eggs, well beaten
>1 teaspoon vanilla
>1½ cups sifted cake flour
>½ teaspoon salt
>1 teaspoon baking powder

Mix well. Spread in a 13x9x2-inch pan.

Beat until stiff:
>1 egg white

Add:
>1 cup brown sugar.

Continue beating and fold in:
>½ cup chopped nuts.

Spread over mixture in pan. Bake at 375° for 25 minutes. Cut into squares when cool.

>*Joan E. Smith*
>DETROIT

Rum Raisin Brownies II

(Just a unique concoction of well-chosen substitutions from depleted kitchen cupboards. This is how I have always cooked–with the bare minimum.)

¾ cup granulated sugar
1 stick (¼-pound),
    plus 2 tablespoons butter or margarine
6 level tablespoons cocoa
½ cup flour
2 eggs
1/8 teaspoon baking powder
1 teaspoon rum extract
½ cup chocolate coated raisin candies (Raisinettes)
½ cup chopped walnuts

Mix eggs and sugar. Melt butter or margarine in saucepan over medium heat, and stir in cocoa until smooth. Blend two mixtures together; stir in remaining ingredients (except Raisinettes and nuts), beginning with the flour, until all are combined. Lastly, fold in raisinettes and nuts. Do not overmix.

Bake at 350° in 10x7x1½-inch pan for about 25 minutes, or until top springs back and brownies pull from sides of pan.

Cool completed; dust lightly with powdered sugar. No need for icing. Do not refrigerate. Cut in very small squares.

Makes 24.

Agnes Riordan-Gira
Detroit

Surprise Brownies

¼ cup oil
½ cup brown sugar
1 egg
¾ cup flour
1 teaspoon baking powder
¼ teaspoon salt
½ teaspoon almond flavoring
¼ cup candied fruit peel
⅓ cup sesame seeds

Blend oil and sugar. Add egg and beat together.
Combine flour, salt, and baking powder. Add to first mixture.
Stir in almond flavoring, fruit and seeds.
Spread evenly into a greased 8x8x2-inch pan. Bake at 350° about 25
minutes. Cut into 16 squares when slightly cool.

Miriam Schweitzer
OAK PARK

Chocolate Cheesecake Brownies

(My mother made these when I was young and I made them for my fou children. They were always delicious.)

Cheesecake Batter

2 tablespoons butter
¼ cup sugar
½ teaspoon vanilla
1 tablespoon cornstarch
¾ cup cottage cheese (sieved)
1 egg
½ teaspoon lemon juice

Chocolate Batter

3 ounces unsweetened chocolate
¼ cup (½ stick) butter
2 eggs
1 cup sugar
½ cup unsifted flour
½ teaspoon baking powder
½ teaspoon salt
½ cup chopped nuts
1 teaspoon vanilla
½ teaspoon almond extract

Prepare cheesecake batter:
Cream butter and sugar together; beat in vanilla. Add cornstarch, cottage cheese, egg and lemon juice; beat well. Set aside.
Prepare chocolate batter:
Melt chocolate and butter over hot water; let cool. Beat eggs until thick. Gradually beat in sugar. Stir in chocolate mixture, flour, baking powder and salt. Add nuts, vanilla and almond extract; mix well.
Spread half of chocolate batter in buttered 9-inch square baking pan. Pour cheesecake batter over top. Distribute remaining chocolate batter on top of cheesecake batter. (Do not attempt to cover cheesecake batter completely.) With a spoon swirl the two mixtures together.
Bake in preheated 350° oven for 35-40 minutes. Cut into 16 squares while still warm. Serve with chocolate or vanilla ice cream.

Mrs. Vivian Johnson
HOLLAND

153

৯৬৬৩৯ Mocha Nut Frosted Brownies ৯৬৬৩

(I came up with this recipe by combining two other recipes, because I didn't have all the ingredients for either one on hand. Together I came up with this one, which turned out to be delicious!)

> ¾ cup sifted all-purpose flour
> ½ teaspoon double-acting baking powder
> ¼ teaspoon salt
> 2 tablespoons instant coffee (or slightly less)
> 2¼ squares unsweetened chocolate
> ⅓ cup butter or margarine
> 2 eggs, unbeaten
> 1 cup granulated sugar
> 1 teaspoon vanilla extract
> ¾ cup chopped walnuts

Start heating oven to 375°. Grease an 8x8x2-inch pan.

1. Sift together flour, baking powder, salt and coffee.
2. In double boiler, over hot, *not boiling water*, melt chocolate with butter; cool.
3. In bowl, beat eggs with sugar until very light and fluffy; add to chocolate mixture and blend well.
4. Stir flour mixture into chocolate mixture until blended; add vanilla and ½ cup nuts, and gently mix. Pour into pan.
5. Bake 25 minutes, or until center springs back when lightly pressed. Cool; cut into squares after frosting (optional). `

Brownie Frosting

> 1 6-ounce package semi-sweet chocolate pieces
> 1 cup sifted confectioners sugar
> ⅓ cup evaporated milk, undiluted

Melt chocolate over hot, not boiling, water. Add sugar and evaporated milk. Beat until smooth.

Frosts two batches of brownies. Sprinkle tops with **remaining nut** from recipe.

Joanna Lynn Combs
WYANDOTTE

Norwegian Brownies

(My mother's cakes were unusually heavy and moist, so her brownies were chewy and moist–our favorite snack. Cardamom, which was a familiar flavor to us, was used even in her breads.)

> 4 eggs
> 1 cup butter or margarine, melted
> 2 cups sugar
> 2 cups flour
> 2 teaspoons almond flavoring
> 1/8 teaspoon cardamom (ground)

Beat eggs until light. Add sugar, butter, flour, flavoring and cardamom.

DO NOT grease pan. Pour into a 9x13-inch pan. Sprinkle with topping. Bake at 325° for about 45 minutes. Cut when cool.

Topping:

> ½ package (about 2½ ounces) sunflower seeds
> ¼ cup sugar

Toss about and sprinkle on batter.

> Mrs. Ida Henkel
> FLAT ROCK

Brownies with Brown
••••••••••and White Topping ••••••••••

(This is one of our favorite brownie recipes, but we usually only make it for special occasions. One of my 4-H friends gave me the recipe a few years ago.)

> **4 squares of unsweetened chocolate (4 ounces)**
> **⅔ cup butter**
> **2 cups sugar**
> **4 eggs**
> **1½ cups sifted flour**
> **1 teaspoon baking powder**
> **1 teaspoon salt**
> **1 cup nuts**

Heat oven to 350°. Melt chocolate and butter over hot water. Beat in sugar and eggs. Sift dry ingredients together; stir in, along with nuts at the same time. Spread in a greased 9x13-inch pan. Bake 30-35 minutes, until top has a dull crust. Cool.

White Topping

Melt ½ **cup butter** over medium heat. Blend with **4 cups sifted confectioners sugar**. Blend in **4 teaspoons cream** or **milk** and **2 teaspoons vanilla.** Spread on cooled brownies. (This is very stiff.)

Brown Topping

Melt **2 squares unsweetened chocolate (2 ounces)** and **2 tablespoons butter**. When cooled, spread very thin coating over icing.
Scrumptious!

Joanne K. Atkinson
MIDLAND

••••••••••

Butterscotch-Banana Brownies

Cream together:
>   **⅔ cup butter**
>   **1 1-pound box brown sugar (2 cups)**

Add:

>   **2 eggs, slightly beaten**

Add:

>   **3 teaspoons baking powder**
>   **3½ cups flour**
>   **1 teaspoon salt**
>   **1 teaspoon vanilla**
>   **½ cup chopped nuts**
>   **2 mashed ripe bananas**

Mix well.

Add:

>   **6 ounces butterscotch chips**

Spread in greased 10x13-inch pan. Bake at 350° 40 minutes. (If using a 9x13-inch pan, bake 50-60 minutes.)

Joyce A. Skindell
WESTLAND

Disappearing Marshmallow Brownies

Melt in 3-quart saucepan:
> ½ cup butterscotch pieces
> ¼ cup oleo

Add:
> ⅓ cup packed brown sugar
> ¾ cup flour
> 1 teaspoon baking powder
> ¼ teaspoon salt
> ½ teaspoon vanilla
> 1 egg

Add and fold into mixture:
> 1 cup miniature marshmallows
> 1 cup chocolate chips
> ½ cup chopped nuts

Pour into a 9-inch greased square pan. Bake at 350° for 20-25 minutes.

Mina DeKraker
HOLLAND

Mandarin Brownies

(There's an ice cream somewhere called Mandarin Chocolate. The taste unique. Not being an ice creamer, Mandarin Brownies was as close as I ould come! I have three children, a husband and run a day care–everyone is brownie connoiseur, and through countless trials, these were the favorites.)

½ cup shortening
½ cup cocoa
2 eggs (beaten)
1 cup sugar
½ cup orange marmalade
1 cup flour
½ teaspoon soda
1/8 teaspoon salt
½ teaspoon baking powder
½ cup black walnuts
1 teaspoon vanilla

Melt shortening; add cocoa. Add eggs and sugar; beat. Add armalade–beat well. Add flour, soda, salt and baking powder. Beat. dd walnuts and mix well. Stir in vanilla. Pour into a greased and oured pan. Bake for 25 minutes at 350°.

Peggy Day
MARQUETTE

Pan Brownies

(When making up this recipe, I thought of a quick way to mix them up. Everyone who tasted these liked the mixture of several flavors. And, since most people like their brownies fudge-like, I made these quite fudgy by leaving the leavening out.)

In quart saucepan on simmer, melt **2 ounces unsweetened chocolate** and **1 stick butter.** Cool 5 minutes. Stir in **1 cup granulated sugar,** ¼ **teaspoon vanilla extract,** ¼ **teaspoon almond extract** and ¼ **teaspoon French's black walnut (imitation) flavor.**
Beat in **2 eggs,** one at a time, beating until thick and shiny after each addition.
Add ½ **cup sifted all-purpose flour** that has had ¼ **teaspoon salt** sifted with it. Add ½ **cup chopped walnut meats,** ½ **cup chopped, pitted dates** and ½ **cup flaked coconut.** Blend thoroughly; with rubber scraper, spread into a shiny, 8x8x2-inch pan–grease bottom only.
Bake at 350° for 22 minutes. (If you use a Baker's Secret pan, reduce heat to 325°.)
Cool completely in pan before cutting into 16 squares.

Zita Frances Hughes
WILLIS

✿✿✿ Banana Split Brownies ✿✿✿

⅔ cup shortening
1½ cups sugar
4 eggs
1 teaspoon vanilla
1½ cups flour
1 teaspoon baking powder
½ teaspoon salt
2 ounces unsweetened chocolate,
   melted and cooled
1 small banana, mashed
¼ cup strawberry preserves

Melt shortening. Remove from heat; mix in sugar, eggs and vanilla. Add flour, baking powder and salt.

Divide batter in half; add cooled chocolate to one half and mix to remaining half plain batter. Divide this in half, adding mashed banana to one half, strawberry preserves to the other.

Drop batter alternately into greased and floured 9x9-inch baking pan. Run knife through batter several times to marbleize. Bake at 350° 30 minutes, or till done.

Cool and serve with:

Caramel Peanut Sauce

In small saucepan, melt **28 caramels** with ¼ **cup water** over low heat, stirring until sauce is smooth. Add ⅓ **cup chunky peanut butter**; continue stirring until all is combined.

Remove from heat and spoon warm sauce over cooled brownies. Immediately cut into bars, cool and serve.

Rose Adams
DETROIT

161

Rocky Road Brownies with Creamy Fudge Frosting

Brownies:

2 cups sugar
4 eggs
1 cup butter or margarine (softened)
4 envelopes (4 ounces) Nestle's Choco-bake
2 teaspoons vanilla
1⅓ cups flour (unsifted)
1 teaspoon baking powder
1 teaspoon salt
1 cup chopped nuts
1 cup miniature marshmallows
⅔ cup Nestle's butterscotch chips
⅔ cup Reese's peanut butter chips

Preheat oven to 350°.

In mixing bowl, combine sugar, eggs, butter or margarine, Choco-bake and vanilla; beat until creamy. Add flour, baking powder and salt. Mix well.

Carefully fold in nuts, marshmallows, butterscotch chips and peanut butter chips.

Spread in 13x9-inch pan. Bake at 350° for 30-40 minutes until done. Cool completely. Spread with Creamy Fudge Frosting.

(This recipe came about when Diane made her own modifications of a great recipe she had on hand. And, from what people tell her, these brownies can't be beat. It's her personal favorite because, just like a painting, it's Diane's original work of art.)

Creamy Fudge Frosting

2 egg yolks
4 tablespoons butter or margarine (melted)
2 envelopes (2 ounces) Nestle's Choco-bake
1 teaspoon milk
1 teaspoon vanilla
2 cup confectioners sugar (sifted)

Combine egg yolks, butter or margarine, Choco-bake, milk and vanilla. Mix until blended. Gradually add confectioners sugar; beat until creamy.

Note: Recipe may be divided in half

Diane Louise Waddell
BIG RAPIDS

Chocolate Coconut Almond Bars

⅔ cup flour
½ teaspoon baking powder
¼ teaspoon salt
2 eggs
1 cup sugar
⅓ cup butter or margarine, softened
¼ cup coconut
½ teaspoon almond extract
2 squares (2 ounces) unsweetened chocolate, melted

Sift flour, baking powder and salt together. Beat eggs and sugar. Add in butter. Gradually add flour mixture. Pour ½ cup of the batter into a small bowl and mix with coconut and almond extract.

Add chocolate to remaining batter and mix well. Spread in a buttered 8-inch square pan. Drop coconut mixture by teaspoons onto chocolate batter, spreading carefully to form a thin layer.

Bake at 350° for 25-30 minutes.

Cool. Cut into bars.

Makes about 20.

Marbled Peanut Butter-Cheese Brownies

Blend together well:
   ¾ cup cottage cheese
   ¾ cup sugar
   ½ cup brown sugar
   1 stick margarine

Add and blend well:
   2 eggs
   1 teaspoon vanilla

Mix together and add to above:
   1 teaspoon baking powder
   1¼ cups flour
   ½ teaspoon salt
   ¼ cup wheat germ

Mix ingredients well. Spread ¾ of batter in a 9-inch square pan.

To remaining batter add:
   6 tablespoons cocoa
   3 tablespoons soft margarine
   ¼ cup peanut butter
   2 tablespoons milk

Drop by spoonfuls on batter, and marble. Bake 40-50 minutes at 350°. Cool. Dust with powdered sugar.

Patricia Markiecki
WYANDOTTE

Chocolate Scotch Brownies

(This recipe is my own. Everyone who tastes these likes them.)

⅔ cup flour
½ teaspoon baking soda
⅓ cup margarine
2 ounces unsweetened chocolate
2 eggs
1 cup sugar
1 teaspoon vanilla
½ cup chopped walnuts
½ cup butterscotch chips

Preheat oven to 350°. Stir flour and baking powder together and set aside. Melt butter and chocolate over very low heat or in top of double boiler. Let cool.

In mixing bowl, beat eggs; add sugar gradually, beating until eggs are thick and yellow. Stir in chocolate mixture. Add flour mixture and beat well. Add vanilla and nuts, stirring in well. Bake in a greased 8x8x2-inch pan 25 minutes.

During the last 10 minutes of baking, sprinkle the brownies with butterscotch chips and finish baking.

Allan Faye Swan
WESTLAND

🐢 Double Chocolate Marshmallow 🐢 Brownies

(This is a favorite school treat that my children often take for birthdays. At my son's high school graduation open house they were the first food item we ran out of.)

½ cup butter or margarine
¾ cup sugar
2 eggs
1 teaspoon vanilla
¾ cup flour
¼ teaspoon baking powder
¼ teaspoon salt
2 tablespoons baking cocoa
½ cup nuts (optional)

Cream butter and sugar. Beat in eggs and vanilla. Stir together flour, cocoa, baking powder, salt and nuts. Combine with egg mixture. Spread in a greased 9x13-inch pan. Bake at 350° for 15-20 minutes.

Sprinkle **3 cups tiny marshmallows** evenly over top of brownies and bake 3 minutes more or until melted.

Cool and frost with:

6-ounce package chocolate chips
1 cup peanut butter
½ cup nuts (optional)
1½ cups Rice Krispies cereal

In saucepan, combine chocolate chips and peanut butter; cook until chocolate is melted. Stir in cereal and spread on top of cooled brownies.

Alice M. Schafer
ITHACA

Weight Watcher's Brownies

(This recipe was shared at my Weight Watcher's class in Romeo. I don't know where it originated, but my family really enjoys it. Since one serving can be equated on the WW program, it offers the chance for me to enjoy sweets, too.)

   6 envelopes Alba 66 (cocoa mix)
   ⅓ cup flour
   3 mashed medium bananas (well-ripened)
   2 teaspoons vanilla
   2½ teaspoons baking powder
   ¼ cup brown sugar twin
   4 tablespoons coconut (optional)

Mix together and bake in a 9x9-inch pan which has been sprayed with Pam. Bake 15-20 minutes.

Makes 6 servings. Each serving = 1 milk, 1 fruit, ⅓ bread and 2 extras (if coconut is used).

Rosemary Kause
ALMONT

∽∽∽Cocoa-Walnut Brownie Loaf ∽∽∽

¾ cup butter or margarine, softened
¾ cup packed brown sugar
1 teaspoon vanilla
2 eggs
1¾ cups flour
½ cup cocoa
1 teaspoon baking powder
½ teaspoon baking soda
1 8-ounce container of plain yogurt
    at room temperature*
1 cup walnuts, coarsely chopped

*Two-thirds cup of milk can be substituted for yogurt. When using milk, omit baking soda.

Combine butter, sugar and vanilla. Add eggs, one at a time, beating until mixture is light and fluffy. Combine dry ingredients. Add to creamed mixture in thirds alternately with yogurt (or milk). Stir in chopped walnuts.

Pour into greased and floured loaf pan. Bake 65-75 minutes, or until cake springs back when lightly touched with fingertip. (Top may be cracked.)

Cool in pan 10 minutes. Invert onto wire rack and cool completely.

Frost with Cocoa Fudge Frosting.

Cocoa Fudge Frosting

¼ cup butter or margarine, melted
¼ cup cocoa
1½ cups powdered sugar (may need more for spreading consistency)
3 tablespoons milk
½ teaspoon vanilla
Walnuts, coarsely chopped

Combine all ingredients, except walnuts. Add more powdered sugar, if needed, for spreading consistency. After cake is frosted, decorate top with walnuts.

JoEllen Bollman
BAY CITY

Brownie Crunch Bar

2 sticks oleo, melted
2 cups sugar
6 tablespoons cocoa
2 teaspoons vanilla
4 eggs
1 cup flour
½ teaspoon salt

Cream first four ingredients. Beat in eggs; add flour and salt. Pour into 15½x10½-inch greased pan. Bake at 350° 25 minutes.

While still hot spread a **7-ounce jar of marshmallow cream** on top.

Topping

1 cup crunchy peanut butter
6 ounces chocolate chips
6 ounces butterscotch chips
3 cups Rice Krispies

Melt first three ingredients. Stir in Rice Krispies. Spread on top of brownies.

Julie L. Kempker
HOLLAND

❧ Double Chocolate Brownies ❧

4 eggs
2 cups sugar
1⅓ cups oil
2 cups flour
½ teaspoon salt
1 teaspoon baking powder
4 squares bakers chocolate (melted)
1 cup nuts
2 teaspoons vanilla

Beat eggs; add sugar, then oil. Sift in flour mixed with salt and baking powder. Add melted chocolate, vanilla and nuts. Bake in greased 9x12-inch pan for 35 minutes in 350° preheated oven.

Fudge Icing:

1½ cups sugar
7 tablespoons milk
¼ cup butter or margarine
2 ounces unsweetened chocolate
1 tablespoon corn syrup
¼ teaspoon salt (optional)

In saucepan, cut chocolate in small pieces. Add rest of ingredients. Bring to a rolling boil, stirring constantly. Boil 1 minute. Cool. Add **1 teaspoon vanilla**. Beat until thick.
Spread on brownies and ENJOY!!!!!!

Helen Fillhart
HARRISON

Dainty Tea Brownies

(My mother taught me this recipe–along with several others–when I was only 12 years old. I used to make the brownies for my brothers and sisters, and they only lasted a couple of minutes.

1. Melt together over hot water:
–2 squares (2 ounces) unsweetened chocolate
–⅓ cup shortening

2. Beat in:
–1 cup sugar
–2 eggs

3. Sift together and stir in:
–¾ cup sifted Gold Medal flour
–½ teaspoon baking powder
–½ teaspoon salt

4. Mix in:
–½ cup finely chopped nuts

Spread dough in two well-greased 13x9-inch pans. Sprinkle with **¾ cup blanched and finely sliced green pistachio nuts**. Bake 7 to 8 minutes at 350°.

Cut immediately into squares or diamonds. Remove from pan while warm.

Edward A. Reckinger
DEARBORN

172

Layered Brownies

(When you eat these, it's like eating one of those famous candy bars-- only more of it.)

      ½ pound oleo
      1 ¼ cup sugar
      3 tablespoons cocoa
      1 cup flour
      3 eggs
      1 cup chopped nuts

Mix above ingredients and bake 20 minutes at 350° in a 9x13-inch pan. Remove from oven and spread on **2 cups flaked coconut** and **1 can Eagle brand milk**.

Bake 15-20 minutes longer. When cool, frost with **1 tablespoon oleo, 1 melted chocolate square,** and **1¼ cups 10x sugar.**

Mary V. Conner
MONROE

Cloud Nine Brownies

Melt:

      ½ cup butter or margarine
      1 square (1 ounce) chocolate

Add:

      1 cup sugar
      1 cup all purpose flour mixed with
      1 teaspoon baking powder
      2 beaten eggs
      1 teaspoon vanilla
      ½-1 cup chopped nuts (walnuts or pecans)

Mix well. Spread in greased and floured 9x13-inch pan.
Spread this filling over top of chocolate mixture:

Combine:

      6 ounces cream cheese, softened (buy 8-ounce size)
      ½ cup sugar
      2 T flour
      ¼ cup butter or margarine (softened)
      1 beaten egg
      ½ teaspoon vanilla

Blend until smooth. Add **¼ cup chopped nuts** and spread on chocolate mixture.

Sprinkle **1 cup chocolate chips** over top. Bake at 350° 25-35 minutes until toothpick or tester is clean when inserted.

Sprinkle with **2 cups miniature marshmallows**. Bake 2 minutes longer.

While brownies are baking, melt in a large saucepan:
   ¼ cup margarine
   1 square (1 ounce) chocolate
   2 ounces cream cheese (remaining from 8 ounces)
   ¼ cup milk
Add:
   1 teaspoon vanilla
   1 box (1 pound) powdered sugar (3¾ cups)

Beat until smooth. Pour immediately over hot brownies and marshmallow topping. Swirl frosting together.

Robie Laughlin
PORT HURON

🌺 Two Mothers' Brownies 🌺

(This recipe is one of our favorites. The brownie recipe is from my mother-in-law, and the frosting recipe is from my mother. So, it is truly a marriage made in heaven.)

1 cup sugar
2 eggs
½ cup flour
¼ teaspoon salt
1 teaspoon vanilla
1 cup chopped nuts
2 squares baking chocolate
¼ pound butter

Melt butter and chocolate together in small saucepan over low flame. Cream eggs and sugar. Add sifted flour and salt. Add vanilla and chopped nuts. Lastly add butter melted with chocolate. Bake in 400° oven for 15-20 minutes. When cool, frost with chocolate frosting as described below.

Frosting

1½ tablespoons butter
1½ squares baking chocolate
2 tablespoons hot milk
1 cup powdered sugar
1/8 teaspoon salt
1 teaspoon vanilla

Melt butter and chocolate together in small saucepan over low flame. Combine sifted powdered sugar and salt in small bowl. Pour in hot milk and stir to dissolve completely. Add vanilla and the chocolate mixture. Frosting will be very thin. Beat while hot until it thickens enough to spread.

Carol Weisfeld
DETROIT

Upside-Down Brownies

1 cup semi-sweet chocolate chips
2/3 cup Eagle Brand condensed milk
1 teaspoon vanilla
1/2 cup chopped walnuts
1/4 cup coconut
1 box brownie mix (enough for 9x13-inch pan)

In top of double boiler, melt chocolate chips. Stir in condensed milk, vanilla, nuts and coconut.

Pour into a 13x9-inch pan lined with wax paper.

Prepare brownie mix according to directions on package.

Pour gently over mixture in pan.

Bake brownies according to package directions. Invert brownies on rack and remove pan. Let stand 10 minutes. Remove wax paper. Cool.

Cut into 2 dozen, 2-inch squares.

Orange-Molasses Brownies

2 eggs
1 cup sugar
1 cup light molasses
½ cup oil
2 teaspoons grated orange peel
2 cups flour
1 teaspoon salt
½ teaspoon soda
2 cups (12 ounces) chocolate chips

Beat eggs. Beat in sugar, molasses, oil and orange peel. Stir in flour, salt and soda. Add chocolate chips. Pour into an oiled 9x12-inch pan. Bake at 350° for 35-40 minutes.

Dee Moline
Cheboygan

Peanut Butter Chip Brownies

(I like this recipe because the Dream Whip keeps the brownies soft. Using ½ carob powder and ½ baking cocoa, gives these brownies an interesting flavor.)

½ cup shortening or 1 stick margarine
1 cup sugar
2 eggs
¾ cup flour
½ teaspoon baking powder
½ teaspoon salt
¼ cup baking cocoa
¼ cup carob powder
2 tablespoons Dream Whip (powder)
½ cup peanut butter chips
½ cup chopped nuts (optional)

Heat oven to 350°. Grease square pan, 8x8x2 inches. Melt margarine. Beat in sugar and eggs. Blend together all dry ingredients; stir in. Mix in peanut butter chips and nuts.

Spread in pan. Bake 30-35 minutes. Cool slightly and cut into squares. Makes 16 2-inch squares. Great plain or you can frost with your favorite frosting.

Sharyn Nelsen
WAYNE

Peanut Butter 'n Chocolate Brownies

3 cups sifted all-purpose flour
1 tablespoon baking powder
¾ cup, plus 2 tablespoons peanut butter
½ cup butter
2¼ cups sugar
1 cup packed brown sugar
1½ teaspoons vanilla
1 package (4-ounce size) vanilla instant
   pudding mix
4 eggs
¼ cup chopped chocolate-covered peanuts
3 ounces unsweetened chocolate,
   melted and cooled
½ cup peanut butter chips
½ cup semi-sweet chocolate pieces

Mix flour with baking powder. Cream the peanut butter, butter, sugars, vanilla and the dry instant pudding mix. Beat in eggs. Gradually add flour mixture. Stir in peanuts.

Divide batter in half; add chocolate and mix into one half. Drop batters alternately into greased 9x13-inch baking pan.

Bake at 350°.

After baking for 35 minutes, sprinkle the chips over warm brownies. Let softed. Spread to cover top and marbleize.

Rose Adams
DETROIT

Fudge Brownie Muffins

2 cups salted butter
8 ounces unsweetened baking chocolate
3½ cups sugar
2 cups all purpose flour
8 eggs
2 teaspoons vanilla
4 cups coarsely chopped walnuts or pecans
36 walnut or pecan halves

Preheat oven to 300°. Line muffin pans with paper baking cups. Melt butter with chocolate in top of double boiler set over simmering water. Combine sugar and flour in a large bowl. Stir in chocolate mixture. Add eggs and vanilla. Stir till just blended. (Do not overmix.)

Spoon into muffin cups to ⅔ full level. Top each with a walnut or pecan half. Bake until tester inserted in center comes out clean–about 40 minutes. Cool on racks.

Makes 36.

Mary Christopher
DEARBORN HEIGHTS

Chocolate-Meringue Brownies

1 cup all-purpose flour
¼ teaspoon salt
¼ teaspoon baking soda
½ cup butter or margarine
¾ cup packed brown sugar
2 envelopes (2 ounces) pre-melted unsweetened chocolate
3 eggs
1½ teaspoon vanilla
¼ teaspoons cream of tartar
¾ cup granulated sugar
1 6-ounce package (1 cup) semi-sweet chocolate chips

Stir together flour, salt and baking soda. Set aside.

Beat butter and brown sugar until fluffy.

Mix in pre-melted chocolate.

Separate egg whites from yolks; set whites aside. Add egg yolks and vanilla to batter and mix well.

Gradually beat in flour mixture.

Spread in greased 13x9-inch baking pan. Bake at 350° for 10 minutes.

While brownies are baking, beat egg whites with cream of tartar until soft peaks form. Gradually add the sugar; beat until stiff peaks form.

Remove brownies from oven and sprinkle with chocolate chips while still hot. Spread meringue over chocolate chips.

Return to oven and bake 30 minutes more, or until golden brown.

Cut into bars while warm.

Makes 24.

Coconut-Topped Brownies

1 cup soft butter or margarine
Sugar
3 eggs
1 teaspoon vanilla
4 squares unsweetened chocolate
1 cup sifted flour
½ teaspoon salt
1 cup chopped nuts
½ cup flaked coconut
½ teaspoon cinnamon

Cream ½ cup of the butter.

Add **2 cups sugar** and eggs; beat until light. Add vanilla.

Melt remaining ½ cup butter with the chocolate; cool. Beat into first mixture.

Add sifted flour and salt, and nuts. Mix well.

Pour into greased and floured 9x13x2-inch pan. Sprinkle with **2 tablespoons sugar**, coconut and cinnamon, mixed.

Bake in 350° oven about 45 minutes.

Cool in pan; cut into 1½-inch squares.

Makes 60.

Doris Sprague
LIVONIA

Surprise Brownies

(I often take a basic recipe and start adding my own ingredients. This is how I came up with "Surprise Brownies." Little kids really love them because of all the little surprises in each bite (raisins, chocolate chips, and marshmallows); all topped with chocolate frosting.

> 1 stick margarine, softened
> 1 cup sugar
> 2 eggs, unbeaten
> 1 teaspoon vanilla
> 4 tablespoons cocoa
> 1 cup all-purpose flour
> ½ teaspoon salt
> ½ teaspoon baking powder
> 2 tablespoons milk
> ½ cup raisins
> ½ cup semi-sweet chocolate chips
> 1 cup miniature marshmallows

Preheat oven to 325°.
Grease a 9-inch square pan.
Combine margarine, sugar, eggs and vanilla, mixing well.
Sift together cocoa, flour, salt and baking powder.
Add to creamed mixture.
Stir in milk, thoroughly blending.
Fold in raisins, chocolate chips and marshmallows. Spread in pan and bake 25 minutes.
Cool and frost.

Frosting for Surprise Brownies

> 4 tablespoons margarine, softened
> 4 tablespoons cocoa
> 2 cups confectioners sugar
> 4-5 tablespoons evaporated milk
> Dash salt
> 1 teaspoon vanilla

Sift together dry ingredients. Add margarine, vanilla and evaporated milk. Beat until creamy.
Spread on brownies.

Brenda S. Black
HOWELL

184

Favorite Graham-Mallow Bars

10-ounce package large marshmallows,
  snipped into small pieces
1 cup sugar
1 cup evaporated milk
3 ounces unsweetened chocolate
1 teaspoon vanilla
3 cups graham cracker crumbs
1 cup chopped walnuts

In a heavy saucepan, bring to a boil the marshmallows, sugar, milk and chocolate; stir constantly. Boil, stirring, for 5 more minutes. Remove from heat and mix in vanilla, graham cracker crumbs and walnuts.

Spread in greased 9-inch square dish. Chill until firm.

Cut with sharp knife dipped in hot water.

Devilish Delights

(These brownies are gone before they have a chance to cool. The brownie consists of three layers. One is a cookie crust. Next is the dark brownie with walnuts or pecans. The top layer is a cream cheese swirl layer.)

Cookie Crust:

1½ cups sifted flour
¼ cup, plus 2 tablespoons sugar
1½ teaspoons lemon juice
1½ teaspoons vanilla
2 egg yolks (save whites for cream cheese layer)
¾ cup softened margarine or butter

Mix all ingredients by hand or fork. Pat into the bottom and up the sides of a 10-inch pie plate. Cover the edge of the pie plate with foil to protect the crust edge from browning. Preheat oven to 400° and bake for 10 minutes.

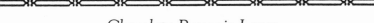

Chocolate Brownie Layer:

3 eggs
1½ cup sugar
¾ cup margarine or butter
¾ cup flour
½ cup unsweetened cocoa
1½ teaspoons vanilla
¾ cup chopped walnuts or pecans

Melt butter and set aside. In bowl combine beaten eggs and sugar. Mix together. Add cocoa to butter and mix. Then add to sugar mixture. Stir in flour and vanilla. Add chopped nuts. Let stand for 10 minutes.

Cream Cheese Layer:

3 ounces of cream cheese, softened
2 egg whites
1 teaspoon vanilla
½ cup confectioners sugar
Milk

In food processor or blender, cut cheese into small pieces. Place in blender. Add egg whites and vanilla. Beat for 30 seconds. Add confectioners sugar. Blend for 30 seconds. Add enough milk to be able to pour the mixture on top of the brownie mixture.

Take crust and pour brownie mixture into it.

Take cream cheese mixture and, with a spoon, ladle it onto the top, creating a swirl.

Preheat oven to 350°. Have a pan larger than the pie plate with water heating in it. Once the water is heated, place the pie plate into the water. Let bake for 30-40 minutes. Towards the end of baking time you may want to place foil around the edge to protect the crust.

Let cool. Slice and serve.

Debbie Grant
Novi

Triple Layer Brownies

> 1 12-ounce package (2 cups) Nestle semi-sweet chocolate
>   morsels (divided)
> 1 6-ounce package (1 cup) Nestle butterscotch morsels
> 2 cups unsifted flour
> 1½ teaspoons baking powder
> ½ teaspoon salt
> 1 cup soft butter
> 1 cup brown sugar, firmly packed
> 2 teaspoons vanilla extract
> 3 eggs
> 1 cup chopped nuts

Preheat oven to 350°.

Over hot water, melt 1 cup semi-sweet chocolate morsels. Set aside.

In another saucepan, melt over hot water the butterscotch morsels. Set aside.

In small bowl, combine flour, baking powder, and salt. Set aside.

In large bowl, combine butter, brown sugar and vanilla; beat until creamy. Add eggs, one at a time, beating well after each addition. Blend in flour mixture. Stir in nuts.

Divide batter in half. Blend melted butterscotch morsels into first half. Spread into well-greased 13x9x2-inch pan.

Blend melted chocolate morsels into second half and spread evenly over butterscotch layer. Bake at 350° for 35 minutes.

Remove from pan; sprinkle remaining 1 cup chocolate morsels evenly over top of brownies. Let morsels set about 5 minutes until soft. Spread evenly on top of brownies. Cool completely and cut into 2x1-inch bars.

Makes 4 dozen.

Loretta Hadjantoni
WARREN

Dessert Brownies

(This recipe was shared with me by Janet Zerull, formerly of this area, and now living in Fort Wayne, Indiana. She is a super cook and a great friend.)

1 box brownie mix for 9x13-inch pan (I use Kroger's.)
1 13-ounce jar Kraft Marshmallow Creme
1 6-ounce package chocolate chips
1 cup peanut butter
2 cups Special K
2 eggs
⅓ cup water

Mix and bake brownies following package directions (using eggs and water) in a 9x13-inch pan. Then put Marshmallow Creme on top. Put in oven 1 minute. Take it out and try to spread, put it back in the oven 1 minute, try to spread, etc. until top is covered.

Melt chocolate chips. Add peanut butter and Special K. Spread over top a little at a time. Cool very thoroughly and cut into squares.

Gooey, but great!

Maureen Vollmer
LIVONIA

Other Eberly Press Books

Michigan Cooking...and Other Things A unique collection of recipes based on Michigan's agriculture, witty articles by Michigan writers, and pen and ink drawings of Michigan points of interest. Fun to read and a practical addition to anyone's cookbook collection. $4.95

More Michigan Cooking...and Other Things More of the same. $4.95

Our Michigan: Ethnic Tales & Recipes Interested in recipes for Canadian butter tarts, Polish pierogie, Norwegian meatballs, German apple strudel, Hungarian paprikash, Czech kolache or 150 more ethnic dishes? Curious about the people who settled Michigan from all over the world and their fascinating stories? Like historical photos? Then, this is the book for you. $6.95

101 Apple Recipes Apple dumplings, apple quiche, paper bag apple pie, crunchy caramel apple pie. You name it...it's here. $2.50

101 Cherry Recipes Cherry bounce, black cherry biscuits, cherry chicken, cherry brandy pie, cherry cheese pie, cherry mousse, cherry jam cake...dozens more. $2.50

eberly press
430 N. HARRISON
E. LANSING, MI 48823

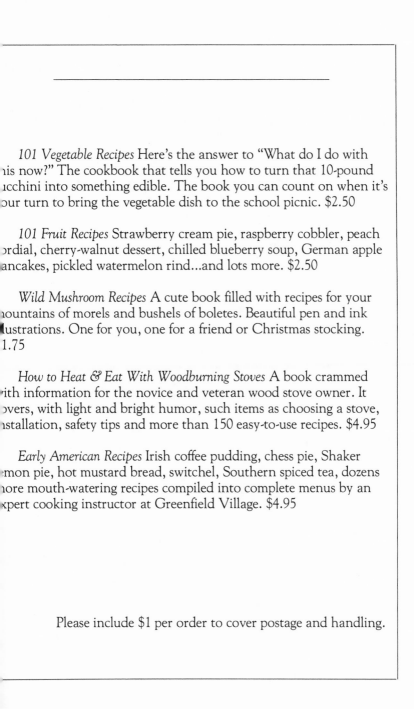

101 Vegetable Recipes Here's the answer to "What do I do with this now?" The cookbook that tells you how to turn that 10-pound zucchini into something edible. The book you can count on when it's your turn to bring the vegetable dish to the school picnic. $2.50

101 Fruit Recipes Strawberry cream pie, raspberry cobbler, peach cordial, cherry-walnut dessert, chilled blueberry soup, German apple pancakes, pickled watermelon rind...and lots more. $2.50

Wild Mushroom Recipes A cute book filled with recipes for your mountains of morels and bushels of boletes. Beautiful pen and ink illustrations. One for you, one for a friend or Christmas stocking. $1.75

How to Heat & Eat With Woodburning Stoves A book crammed with information for the novice and veteran wood stove owner. It covers, with light and bright humor, such items as choosing a stove, installation, safety tips and more than 150 easy-to-use recipes. $4.95

Early American Recipes Irish coffee pudding, chess pie, Shaker lemon pie, hot mustard bread, switchel, Southern spiced tea, dozens more mouth-watering recipes compiled into complete menus by an expert cooking instructor at Greenfield Village. $4.95

Please include $1 per order to cover postage and handling.